Writing Teachers
Writing Software

Advances in Computers and Composition Studies

Series Editors:

Gail E. Hawisher
University of Illinois at Urbana-Champaign

Cynthia L. Selfe
Michigan Technological University

Series Design Editor:

James R. Kalmbach
Illinois State University

*Creating a Computer-Supported Writing Facility:
A Blueprint for Action*

*Evolving Perspectives on Computers and Composition Studies:
Questions for the 1990s*

*Writing Teachers Writing Software:
Creating Our Place in the Electronic Age*

Writing Teachers Writing Software

Creating Our Place in the Electronic Age

Paul J. LeBlanc
Springfield College

With a foreword by
Hugh L. Burns
University of Texas at Austin

NCTE

Computers and Composition

NCTE Editorial Board: Rafael Castillo, Gail Hawisher, Joyce Kinkead, Charles Moran, Louise Phelps, Charles Suhor, Chair, *ex officio*, Michael Spooner, *ex officio*

Interior Design: Adapted from James R. Kalmbach

Production Editor: Michelle Sanden Johlas

Manuscript Editor: Robert A. Heister/Humanities & Sciences Associates

Cover Design: Barbara Yale-Read

NCTE Stock Number: 59117-3050

© 1993 by the National Council of Teachers of English, 1111 W. Kenyon Road, Urbana, Illinois 61801-1096, and by *Computers and Composition,* Michigan Technological University, Houghton, Michigan 49931, University of Illinois at Urbana-Champaign, Urbana, Illinois 61801. All rights reserved. Printed in the United States of America.

Michigan Technological University and the University of Illinois at Urbana-Champaign are equal opportunity educational institutions/ equal opportunity employers.

It is the policy of NCTE in its journals and other publications to provide a forum for the open discussion of ideas concerning the content and the teaching of English and the language arts. Publicity accorded to any particular point of view does not imply endorsement by the Executive Committee, the Board of Directors, or the membership at large, except in announcements of policy, where such endorsement is clearly specified.

Library of Congress Cataloging-in-Publication Data

LeBlanc, Paul, 1957–
    Writing teachers writing software : creating our place in the electronic age / Paul J. LeBlanc ; with a foreword by Hugh L. Burns.
      p. cm. — (Advances in computers and composition studies)
    Includes bibliographical references and index.
    ISBN 0-8141-5911-7
    1. English language—Rhetoric—Study and teaching. 2. English language—Computer-assisted instruction. 3. Computer-assisted instruction—Authorship. I. Title. II. Series.
PE 1404.L43   1993
808'.042'0285416—dc20   93-16808
                                                                                           CIP

*For Emma and Hannah,
and especially for Pat*

Contents

Foreword — xi

Acknowledgments — xix

1. Introduction — 1
   Technology Takes Hold — 3
   Of Teachers and Their Tools — 5
      The Emergence of Computers and Writing Studies — 5
      Faculty-Based Software Development in Composition — 6
      Collecting Stories — 8

2. Understanding Computer Software — 11
   Turning Knowledge into Software — 12
      Procedural Knowledge — 14
      Declarative Knowledge — 16
      Qualitative Knowledge — 16

3. The "Who" and "How" of CAC Software Development — 20
   The Lone Developer Model — 25
   The Small Design Group Model — 34
   The Entrepreneurial Design Group — 42
   Professional Software Development — 52
   The Research-Based Design Team — 57

4. Forces That Impact CAC Software Design 66
Technology 67
  Programming Languages 67
  Object-Oriented Programming 68
  Hypermedia 72
  System Architecture 76
  Networking 79
  CD-ROM 81
  Artificial Intelligence 82
Reward and Recognition 87
Funding 96
Software Publication 98
The Future of CAC Development Models 108
  The Lone Developer 109
  The Small Design Group 112
  The Entrepreneurial Design Group 115
  The Research-Based Design Team 117
  An Overall View 120

5. CAC Software Design and the New Literacy 124
Relying on Corporate Creativity 127
Forging Alliances 130
  Military Funding 133
The Ascendancy of Cognitive Theory in CAC Design 134
  Diversity in Composition Studies 135
  Cognition, Computers, and Composition Studies 137

The Influence of Cognitive-Based CAC Programs	141
Diversity in Cognitive Approaches	143
Giving Shape to the Future: Some Reflections	146
Appendix	153
Works Cited	161
Author	177
Index	179

Foreword

> To some things we by art must needs attain,
> Others by destiny or luck we gain.
>
> —Agathon, cited by Aristotle, *Rhetoric*

For years, the charge for the computer-assisted composition community has been to envision state-of-the-future educational technologies. But did we really know the full significance of what we were about as a community? Most likely we still do not realize how fast the world is changing. These are the best of quantum times; these are the worst of quantum times.

If we thought about how wonderful it would be to provide all schools with a literacy infrastructure upon which to build successful learners, thinkers, and writers, it was accidental. If we wondered how universal connectivity and communication would mean nothing if learners were not equipped well enough to be able to write or read, it was in those long daydreams in our private, computerized inner sanctums, when we were one with the code.

We may not have always realized that the software we were developing would empower students who would need, in their lifetimes, the ability to seek out and retrieve information from any source in the global village. Today, our writers have the capability to link up with other writers who are working on similar projects, either across the hallway or across the globe. They have the capability to write in a community of writers from other countries, only satellite-seconds away. *Carpe technologia.*

Paul LeBlanc's romantic quest makes us all seem smarter than we were. At least, this is how I felt as Paul told me of his wanderings to meet many of you—his friends, all. Here is the most definitive "who's who" in the development of computer-assisted composition over the past fifteen years. Just at the moment when computers and composition studies are gaining more and more popularity and scholarly respect, here comes a scholar who is interested in examining and telling the story so that software developers and teachers of composition can begin to remember.

Here are the powerful patterns and portraits. These are the roots of rhythm in computers, technology, and composition. When Paul asked me to write a foreword for his excursion into the world of software development in composition and the craft of technology-assisted writing, I was curious how his journey would turn out. Now, I know.

Before reading, I would prescribe a dose or two of self-examination. How have you been developing software? How will you develop software in the future? What barriers have you overcome to marry technology and the humanities? Why is it important that composition teachers have a view or an appreciation of software development? Who designs composition software? What trends are emerging in composition software? How can faculty participate in the design and the development of software for composition studies? What are your own models for software development? Can you personally afford or risk tenure in your department? What are the implications for the field of composition and computers? Such an honest self-inventory will better prepare you for a conclusion of connections. LeBlanc will tell you in the end how computer technology "relies on the diminution of its physical presence and is mostly experienced through software, which is created through intellectual endeavor and imagination—the currency of academic life." He is right! "We thus have a rare opportunity," he concludes, "to play a part in our own destiny, to help shape the revolution." The vision is one we must share, as Aristotle recalled Agathon's words: "To some things we by art must needs attain / Others by destiny or luck we gain." In software development, art is better than luck.

The several, revolutionary agendas in this book are grounded in the pursuit of knowledge—for computer technology has a nasty, consistent habit of providing us only enough knowledge to realize what we could be doing with even more technology. The biggest misconception in the arena of current design and development is that we develop finished products. Software does not allow itself to be finished. Software is never finished. That is why software is *soft*. I like to think that many of the people featured here have visions dancing in their heads—about teaching with technology as well as a sometimes unexplainable motivation for building tools for composing, when, in fact, they know better. They know their current tools will not fulfill their future instructional potentials. But they also realize that this is the only road. Happily, others are on the journey as well, although we have not had to worry about a gridlock of scholars.

Let me present three goals for bringing technology into any educational environment and for developing software for composition. What do we want writers and learners to be able to accomplish?

- To use technology to perform some tasks, such as writing a paper, sending a message, responding to an audience.
- To learn about and understand technology, such as how desktop publishing works or how to write the software that implements a grammar-checking program.
- To employ the technology to support instructional goals, such as the use of an integrated writing environment to teach composition in a local-area network classroom.

In tight fiscal times, developers have also had to deal with issues of cost and availability, but the software developers featured here have identified and prioritized educational system needs with a potential for cost-effective resolution through technological innovations. Reaching the three goals of technology—using, learning, and employing—must inform all aspects of our computer-assisted composition designs.

What are the strategies for reaching these goals? Strategies should be designed for students, teachers, and communities *by* students, teachers, and communities. Here are some to consider:

- First, teach how to learn in today's information society—

the key objective of education. Computers are the new medium of knowledge. Through readily accessible computer networks, students can use the electronic libraries of the future.

- Second, achieve instructional gains through the application of technology. The benefits of one-on-one instruction are supported by the research. A composition teacher's role increases significantly as facilitator, coach, and mentor, as a result of increased teaching time. Collaborative learning and writing environments on local area networks are enabling dramatic increases in class participation, by empowering students to become aware of very real audiences—themselves.

- Third, create a global focus through enhanced technological capabilities. Use of technology brings the world into the classroom, breaking down barriers of ethnocentricity and prejudice. Technologies will support distance learning and teleconferencing, providing a means of connecting students and writers across geographical, political, and cultural boundaries.

Developers have had in mind an insertion of technology into the learning environment which emphasizes technology's ability to help improve the teacher-to-student ratio, making one-on-one instruction and team collaboration the standard approaches to teaching and learning. This is strategically possible.

Let me offer a brief reflection on the possible and the impossible. In Book II, Chapter 19 of the *Rhetoric*, Aristotle speaks of the "Possible and Impossible." He argues that, "If it is possible for one of a pair of contraries to be or happen, then it is possible for the other" (1392a, 9–10). He illustrates:

> That if a thing can come into being in a good and beautiful form, then it can come into existence generally; thus a house can exist more easily than a beautiful house. That if the beginning of a thing can occur, so can the end; for nothing impossible occurs or begins to occur. . . . That if the end is possible, so too is the beginning.

Beginnings have compelled the many software developers you

will meet in the following chapters. Our computer-assisted composition programs have come into being generally, but their goodness and their beauty have yet to be truly achieved. That is what we've begun—and if the beginning of a thing can occur, so too can the end.

If LeBlanc has written of past facts, how should we be encouraged to address questions of the future? How should they be argued? Aristotle would have us consider:

> That a thing will be done if there is both the power and the wish to do it; or if along with the power to do it, there is a craving for the result, or anger, or calculation, prompting it. (1392a, 1–3).

If there is a foundation, there will be a house. LeBlanc's notions about computers and writing "redesign" are worth examining in detail. Are we in an age of evolution or revolution in design? These stories illustrate the power and the wish to change the way technology works for us in our composition courses. There continues to be a craving for tools that will empower each individual writer. These teacher-developers are angry about the massive illiteracy. Many have had to resort to political calculation to make their technologically enriched learning places exist. But now there is a foundation. Their mantra: Develop it and they will come.

If these are the stories of how we begin to remember, then what are the lessons for future developers? Here are three I find most promising; you will find others throughout this book:

- Specify a bold technology-support infrastructure. Consider the complete set of information/communication systems technologies such as availability of computers, use and need for local-area networks, availability of word-processing software, extent of satellite and wide-area networks, even television and radio studios, etc. Then design software that will allow access to shared resources with other writers, developers, teachers, schools, communities, and countries.
- Design for overall technology awareness. Develop software that enable individuals to achieve the literacies we will need in the twenty-first century. Especially within the school's

own community, provide role models who are working in and developing the technologies, and acquaint students with common technologies for the new communication age (e.g., networks, common software applications, FAX machines, photocopiers, CD players, video technologies, laser discs, and so on, through hands-on experience).

- Solicit community support and real audiences for computer-assisted writers. For example, writing about a judicial process is best done where the action is. Identify places where situated learning and writing experiences are appropriate and best handled in the real world—then connect.

My hope is that tools such as those dreamt of by the developers in this book will provide avenues for global literacies and universal understandings. If I am disturbed about the future, it is because we may not be able to develop their ideas fast enough to keep pace with the changes in hardware. The gap we experience between just being and just becoming will continue to broaden. These are the evolutions in design and development of computer-assisted composition, and they are to be expected and somehow compensated for.

This book reflects and rekindles many memories. Software development finally boils down to a list of qualities you want to see developed in people. As a teacher, you will not have time to do it all, to do it one-on-one, to do it with swank and gusto and enthusiasm and guts. In my case, I still want to have writers talk about "idea" as a plurality—a great chain of associations, memories, experiences, knowledge, and information. Technology allowed me to get there. We can all build such unique foundations for our writers.

Can you remember the first time you allowed your students to work on a computer in the writing workshop? Were you like me at first, trying to pry into their writing zone and help? When were you brave enough to leave the room and look back in through a window—wondering if the software you had developed was powerful enough to be useful? Are you part of the generation that helped switchboard operators listen to the high-pitched sounds of mainframe computers yearning to be called? Are you part of the generation who told colleagues the differences between hardware and software, bits and bytes, word processing and data processing, hypertension and hypermedia? Can you remember when your composition students began enjoying the composition of an essay, even laughing aloud at different times while writing? Have you noticed, in these settings, how you have provided a place and pace for writing and thinking that honors each student's learning and writing styles? Do you have college-age children who come home at Christmas break and blurt out with excitement, "You would really like the literature class I'm taking. It's cool. We write all at once on a local-area network. Then we share the transcripts!"

Yes, software development is cool.

Yes, we have been and are a community of possibilities. "Good enough" is no longer plausible. Intrepid development. Relentless patience. Whoever thought that electrons and microchips could be such good friends to humanists?

Yes, this is a book about the importance of connecting.

Yes, these are the stories of how we begin to remember the evolution.

Yes, these are the roots and rhythms of the quiet revolution of technology in our composition classrooms.

Yes. Thank you, Paul.

Hugh L. Burns
San Antonio, Texas

Acknowledgments

I began interviewing faculty software designers in 1988, and this work has undergone many changes in the years since. Much of that revision was due to the gentle guidance and wisdom of those wonderful teachers with whom I studied at the University of Massachusetts at Amherst. Charles Moran, who has been a great mentor, brought me into my very first computer writing classroom and has remained at my side ever since, exploring technology and education with the most humane of perspectives. He has been a wise, generous, and good friend. Anne Herrington taught me about research and high standards, and forced me to do my best work for her—and she did so with grace, a sense of humor, and considerable patience. Finally, Peter Elbow brought his wide range of knowledge and native curiosity to my project, and with his characteristic smile of benevolence, urged me to write on.

Gail Hawisher and Cynthia Selfe chose my work for the *Computers and Composition* series, and while that act, alone, was fortunate, even greater for me was the opportunity to work with two of the very best minds in the field. They have been terrific editors, offering guidance, insight, and great positive energy. I would also like to thank Michael Spooner, senior editor at NCTE, for his support of this project and his kind mediation between readers, editorial board members, and me. He helped improve this book without ever making me feel like the process was out of my hands.

My greatest thanks go to the many computer and writing people who gave me their time, thoughts, and comments. In sharing with me their research and their experiences designing or working with software, they made me feel deeply what it is to belong to a community of scholars. They include Mimi Schwartz, Wayne Butler, Fred Kemp, Paul Taylor, Hugh Burns,

Helen Schwartz, Nancy Kaplan, Chris Neuwirth, Earl Woodruff, Dan Burns, Molly Hepler, Bill Wresch, Kim Richardson, Jim Parlett, John Smith, Ron Fortune, and many others.

A person who knows the material in this book at least as well as I do is my student aide, Mary Lonergan, who typed hundreds of pages of transcripts and outlasted one heavy duty transcription machine. Mary shaved ten years off the process of preparing this work and thus saved it from obsolescence.

Most of all, I must acknowledge my wife, Pat, and my daughters, Emma and Hannah. They have been patient and supportive and witness to every stage of this project. I remember holding three-month-old Emma and coding interview transcripts, Hannah joyfully coloring over what was to be a draft sent out in that day's mail, and Pat knowing when to come in, sit, and just listen to the day's progress or frustrations. I will have special fondness for this book and the memories that are bound with its creation.

Paul J. LeBlanc
Springfield College

Chapter 1

Introduction

There is a trap in talking about writing and computers. The trap is to consider writing as a "natural" activity and the computer as a technology that merely serves it. The fallacy asserts that writing is writing, whether it be done with pencil, pen, typewriter, or computer—the intellectual act of composing remaining fundamentally unchanged by the various composing tools we possess. However, as Walter Ong (1982) points out, writing is itself a technology, one that initiated "the reduction of dynamic sound to quiescent space, the separation of the word from the living present, where alone spoken words can exist" (p. 82). The movement from orality to literacy was driven by the adoption of a new technology—writing—a technology no more natural or fixed than any other. Now, with the rapid proliferation of the microcomputer, the technology we know as writing is itself undergoing a transformation, the scope of which might be as important and far-reaching as the earlier shift from spoken to written communication. As Ellen McDaniel (1987) says, in discussing composition software:

> The truly substantial influences of printing, like those of writing, were long in developing but ultimately affected human thought, learning, and expression—the text-maker and the making, not simply the text itself. Now, technology's effect on literacy concerns us again as we inspect the densest technology yet to come between idea and expression, imagination and form, thinker and composer. (p. 139)

In other words, writing is being *redesigned* by the computer in much the same way that the Gutenberg press was said to have redesigned it, with similarly profound implications (Eisenstein, 1979).

As Ong (1982) argues, technologies effect "interior transformations of consciousness, and never more than when they affect the word" (p. 82). When individuals adopt a new tool for writing, they may very well be adopting a new way of thinking about writing, and even a new way of thinking, generally. This is not a new idea. Consider Quintilian's advice to his students in the first-century *Institutio Oratoria*:

> It is best to write on wax, owing to the facility which it offers for erasure, though weak sight may make it desirable to employ parchment by preference. The latter, however, although of assistance to the eye, delays the hand and interrupts the stream of thought, owing to the frequency with which the pen has to be supplied with ink. (Graves, 1984, p. 226)

Our writing tools have always mattered in the way we compose. Technological determinists such as Havelock, Eisenstein, McLuhan, and Ong have illustrated the power of technology to reshape the nature of knowledge and knowledge making.

On the other hand, Nancy Kaplan (1991a) points out that technological determinism can fail to recognize the matrix of social, economic, and ideological forces within which technologies arise, are shaped, and then distributed:

> Tools of inscription embody and construct ideological practices, redefining what exists, what is good, and what is possible to do. But understanding the opportunities and transformations that the tools themselves may offer cannot fully explain or predict their effects on the world. Technologies, after all, arise out of and operate within already existing social, political, and economic relations. (p. 21)

She reminds us that the relationship between technology, with its power to shape culture and society, and society itself and its ideologies, within which technologies are themselves shaped, is a recursive one. We are simultaneously the shapers and the shaped, proactive and reactive. As teachers and researchers of writing, we need to be as sensitive to the development and implementation of writing technologies as was Quintilian; as a field we need to pay much closer attention to, and assert our role in, the development and widespread adoption of the microcomputer as the primary tool for writing in the next millennium. Doing so allows us and our students to be users of technology rather than its victims.

Technology Takes Hold

While precomputer writing technologies developed slowly, their impact occurring over a long period of time, computers have invaded the classroom, workplace, and home with dizzying speed. Just four years after the commercial introduction of the microcomputer, computer-based learning programs were in use in 50 percent of U.S. educational institutions (Chambers and Lewis, 1988, p. 31). According to the Second National Survey of Instructional Uses of School Computers, in the two-year period from 1983 to 1985, the number of computers used in elementary and secondary schools quadrupled from 250,000 to over one million. During that same period, the number of schools introducing computers into the curriculum tripled (Herrmann, 1989, p. 111). Over 95 percent of all public schools now have computers, and the ratio of students to computers continues to close from 92 to 1 in 1983, to a current ratio of about 26 to 1 (COTA 31-4). Fortune 500 companies are already predicting "saturation": one computer per white-collar employee (Debs, 1988, p. 5). And a recent poll revealed that 25 percent of American households now own personal computers and that 70 percent of those computers are being used for schoolwork (Lewis, 1992, p. 48). In educational and work settings, and increasingly at home, the number one use of the microcomputer continues to be for writing. As Charles Moran (1991) asserts, "Computers are here; very few writers would return to the old ways, even if they could do so. Because computers are here, we can't *not* teach student writers in on-line environments" (p. 1).

Software programs designed or appropriated for writing in an on-line environment have, appropriately, seen a corresponding increase in number and sophistication. Simple word-processing programs, their roots in the rudimentary line editors of programming software, have evolved into complex programs that can include spelling, grammar, and style checkers; on-line handbooks; desktop publishing features; and electronic mail capabilities. These programs often have windowing capabilities that allow work on multiple documents, electronic note taking, and easy movement between word processing and other types of programs such as database or graphics software. Complementary programs to aid in writing—such as invention, peer editing, instructor feedback, and outlining programs—are widely available. Moreover, as we struggle to understand the effects of these innovations, at the same time, we see breakthrough developments occurring in hypertext and hypermedia which allow the creation of multimedia documents that link text, video, graphics, and sound in multiple, nonlinear ways. Networking, telecommunications, and large database storage media are providing writers with new, powerful possibilities for collaboration and immediate access to vast amounts of information.

As specialists in writing, in the production and study of texts, we, as a field, must come to grips with the profound changes in written communication which are taking place because of the adoption of the microcomputer as a writing tool. Increasingly, we are able to discern the characteristics of the emerging literacy. Andrea Lunsford, in a paper presented at the 1991 MLA convention, indicates some of these changes:

> In speaking of electronic literacies, I take it as a given that print literacy—the traditional technologies of reading and writing—is in the process of being transformed into a literacy or set of literacies in which text is never fixed or definitive; in which authors are not single authorities (much less stable selves), but always polyvocal; in which "reader" and "writer" as well as "creator" and "critic" regularly merge; in which intellectual property as we have known and defined it is challenged and exclusionary "ownership" impossible; and in which new arts and genres will emerge. (p. 4)

While we remain in the transition period between traditional print literacy and electronic literacy, the speed of that transition, if the last ten years are any indication, will be infinitely faster than the hundreds of years that attended the movement from oral to written literacy.

Of Teachers and Their Tools

Anyone working in composition today must pay at least nodding acceptance to the impact of electronic technology—and ironically, even the most recalcitrant are probably working on computers. That has always been the implicit (and often explicit) message of journals like *Computers and Composition* and conferences such as the annual Computers and Writing Conference. That message has been increasingly echoed elsewhere. Alan McKenzie (1991), for example, urges humanist scholars to get on-line in the MLA's *Profession 91*. Lunsford (1991) stressed this point in her MLA address:

> Video and electronic literacy will affect the way we think about and act in the world. I also believe, however, that it is up to *us* to help decide exactly how these new literacies will affect us. Yet our community has, by and large, refused to accept this responsibility for literacy, leaving it instead to those who want to use electronic literacies for their own ends—primarily business, entertainment, and military purposes. (p. 5)

The need for composition and English studies to play a powerful role in the shaping of electronic literacy is the underlying argument of this book.

The Emergence of Computers and Writing Studies

For more than ten years, a small but growing number of composition researchers and teachers have been attempting to assert their role in shaping electronic literacy. As computers found widespread use in college and university writing programs in the 1980s, composition specialists began studying the relationship between writing and technology. My work, for example, had its roots in my experience as a teacher of writing in a new computer-supported environment. My interest was first sparked by something which I had not seen before in my writing classes: students rushing into the lab, a full ten minutes before the scheduled starting time, and lingering on after class until the next eager students forced them to vacate their work sessions.

Before almost anyone conducted research on the effects of computers on the writing process, everyone working with computers knew one thing: most students are highly motivated to write with computers, good effects or not. Computer-Aided Composition (CAC) instructors like me began to watch more closely the writing behaviors that took place in our computer classrooms, and we began to publish our results in the new computer and writing journals that began to spring up.

In retrospect, those of us who were interested in CAC were looking at tools that were new, powerful, and continually evolving. As Gail Hawisher (1989) noted, our research reflected the confusion and contradictions of an emerging field (p. 64). Take, for example, the contradictory research on the quality of revision when performed on a computer. Burnett (1984), Dalton and Hannafin (1987), Howard Kaplan (1986), Moore (1987), and others argued that the quality of student revision is better when performed on a computer. However, Beesley (1986), Coulter (1986), Duling (1985), Woolley (1985), and others disagreed. Some, such as Cirello (1986), Daiute (1985), and Haas and Hayes (1986) reported mixed results. And yet others, myself included, argued that a writer's predisposition toward revision influences the quality of that revision much more than the computer (LeBlanc, 1988; Hawisher, 1989). Yet, underlying this small but growing body of research was a sense that we were all working with a tool that, when widely adopted, might have a dominant influence on our concepts of text and text production.

Faculty-Based Software Development in Composition

While those cited above were reacting to their students' use of computers for writing, other, perhaps braver, souls were working to make the tool their own. They were the first composition teachers and researchers to design and develop their own software. Their numbers included Hugh Burns, who, as a graduate student at the University of Texas at Austin, wrote an invention program based on Aristotle's *topoi*, Burke's pentad, Young, Becker, and Pike's tagmemics. James Strickland wanted a computer program that would enact some of Peter Elbow's prewriting strategies, found none, and then wrote *FREE* in 1982.

Others, scattered about the country, were also engaged in producing composition software. Their efforts often went unnoticed and unrewarded by their institutions, but they pointed to the one area where the field can actively shape the tools it uses, and thus shape the conception of writing implicit in those tools—the design of software.

The focus of this book is faculty development of software for composition studies. It attempts to describe who is building these writing tools, how they are doing so, how their work is being received, and what is likely to affect their efforts in the future. The discussion, however, does not include a survey of current computer writing programs. While such a survey would be useful, it would not clarify the future of faculty-based software development, for the pace of technological change almost always makes a close look at the present an immediately outdated perspective. There is also little discussion of hardware, a reflection of both the minor role writers' needs have played in hardware development and the fact that hardware development is beyond the reach of even the best-funded and most expert computer and writing specialists. However, these conditions are not true for software.

We may have to live with the hardware produced by Apple, IBM, and other corporate manufacturers; software, however, can be written with far fewer resources. Moreover, it is software that gives hardware its final shape, in the sense that software defines how hardware is used. It is software, for example, that makes a computer network a tool for collaboration or a tool for control and exertion of authority. This is what that small number of faculty software developers have always realized. Finding no published studies of their work, I set out to talk with them about the development of CAC software.

My discussions with faculty software developers confirmed an early notion that how a tool gets built, and who is building that tool, will have important implications for how that tool looks and works. The people who build tools, and their methods for doing so, have great power to define their use. This is particularly true for the computer. The manufacturer of a hammer may intend it to be used for building, but it can be used just as easily for a weapon. A software designer, on the other hand, knows that the grammar-checking program he or she designs can be used for little else. If the designer of a networked collaboration program decides not to include a function which allows the instructor control of or access to students' screens, that designer has limited the use of the network as a social control mechanism.

Collecting Stories

At the heart of my research is a collection of stories that describe the design and development of composition software by CAC specialists. Those interviewed ranged from researchers working in well-supported, well-staffed university settings, to untenured instructors with heavy teaching loads, to academic entrepreneurs attempting to combine their teaching and research with the commercial sale of their software. In each case, their accounts addressed five key areas of inquiry:

1. *Who Designs CAC Software?* Who is involved in the development of the software? If more than one person is involved, how does the group interact? In group efforts, how are the responsibilities and work delegated, if at all?

2. *How Are Programs Completed within a Development Model?* For example, does the effort to develop a program start with a model of writing behavior? Is there field testing during and/or after the development of the program?

3. *What Are the Forces That Impact the Development of CAC Software?* What are the key technological components of software development? How are development projects usually funded? What role, if any, do English departments play in the development effort? Does marketing influence design decisions?

4. *What Trends, if Any, Are Emerging in CAC Software Development?* Are new technologies fundamentally altering software development? Are developer profiles changing? Is the increasing interest in software shown by publishing houses proving supportive or problematic?

5. *What Are the Implications of the Aforementioned Areas of*

Inquiry for the Field of Composition, Generally? Can we begin to see ways in which CAC software might challenge accepted beliefs about good writing and writing behaviors? Do emerging trends in CAC software development favor certain theories of writing over others? What should the role of English departments be in supporting the future development of software programs?

While a wide range of models, or approaches, exists for developing software, four principal ones emerged from the interviews:

the Lone Programmer;

the Small Design Group;

the Entrepreneur;

the Research-Based Design Team.

Accounts illustrating each model answer many of the questions posed above, suggest strengths and weaknesses in each approach, and, taken as a group, offer an overview of the state of software development within our profession.

Moreover, the accounts—with all their drama of people being fired for developing software, or staying up late into the night working on programs, or winning national recognition—bring into sharp focus the larger issues facing English studies and composition professionals as we move toward virtual-age literacy. In chapter 4, I use the collected accounts to identify what seem to be the predominant forces shaping software development within composition. Some of these are technical—for example, the availability of easy-to-use software authoring programs or the impact of object-oriented programming languages. Others include the politics of English departments and their attitudes toward technology, generally, and computers and writing research, specifically—for example, the availability of release time and the treatment of software development in promotion and tenure decisions. Software development is often expensive, and the sources of funding for such efforts may also shape the final product. Some of these forces seem to encourage the faculty development of software; others seem to work against it.

If software development is indeed a primary way for composition specialists to help shape the emerging literacy, we, in the field, must understand these influencing forces, and in some cases, address growing problems related to them. These problems are examined in the final chapter of the book, as the scope of the discussion widens to encompass the larger changes in literacy that are taking place due to the force of technological innovation and the role of composition studies in accommodating and guiding those changes.

This work is an attempt to shed light on where we are and where we might go in the development of composition software. It is an understanding that we lack at present. Composition may become more reactive to technology—notice the increasing number of related journal articles and conference panels, and the job advertisements that include computer and writing experience as desired qualifications. By contrast, there continues to be almost no discussion of software design within the field, and there are alarming indications that the number of faculty software developers in composition is declining, thus making us less proactive in shaping the technology. Such a phenomenon raises Lunsford's (1991) key concerns:

> Who will create and control the programs, the networks (on which many are, ironically, silenced and excluded), the architecture of interactive fiction, the prototypes of virtual reality? And who will train not only the creators but the *interpreters* of these electronic literacies? I want to urge that the answer to these "who" questions had better include *us*. (p. 6)

If we wish to take a proactive role in the shaping of electronic literacy, software design should be as mainstream an activity for composition professionals as teaching a writing class, conducting a research study, or writing an article. Otherwise, we risk leaving the new electronic literacy in the hands of "IBM, Disney, and the U.S. Air Force," as Lunsford warns (p. 5), and relinquishing our proper role as central players in shaping the writing spaces of the future.

Chapter 2

Understanding Computer Software

When writing teachers want to create textbooks, they begin almost immediately by examining the marketplace—what has come before and what is out there now. Key elements in any textbook prospectus are the author's recognition of the competition and her accompanying analysis of how the prospective book will allow the publisher to meet that competition head-on. This sensitivity has a basis in market analysis (i.e., the number of copies that a text is likely to sell), but it also speaks to a tradition in the textbook trade that, in the case of composition, stretches back to the nineteenth century and the shift in focus from oral to written discourse (Connors, 1986, pp. 186–187). The prospective textbook writer might start by walking to a shelf and pulling down textbook after textbook, surveying what has already been done, discovering the conventions of the medium, and so on. The writer might also choose to consult the body of critical literature on textbooks, for example, the work of Stewart, de Beaugrande, Welch, Connors, and Winterowd. Moreover, unlike colleagues in other disciplines, whose training may have included much less writing, the writers of composition textbooks are themselves likely to be competent writers and feel comfortable working with text.

In contrast, consider the challenges confronting the writing teacher who wants to develop software. Computers have only seen extensive use in writing instruction for less than a decade. While there exist dozens of writing-related software programs, their distribution has been spotty and tied to particular hardware configurations. These programs have often gone without updating and no longer run under new operating systems, and much of this software is either uninteresting or of poor quality.

Reviews of software are often hard to find; in particular, there is almost no extant body of critical writing about CAC software development. Indeed, one major aim of the present volume is to help establish a context in which future software developers can situate their efforts. Moreover, those involved with software development in recent years report less camaraderie and sharing among faculty developers than that which characterized the early days of such work (Wresch, 1992, interview; H. Schwartz, 1992, interview).

In addition to a lack of tradition or a body of self-reflective research, prospective CAC software developers must work either directly or indirectly with programming languages in which most have had no training. Joseph Bourque (1983) speaks to this challenge in one of the earliest articles examining the faculty software developer in the humanities:

> In addition to mastery of subject matter and methods, the CAI specialist must learn one or more computer languages, a time-consuming process . . . It often means brushing up on math for people who have had most of their education in the humanities, and, as programmers know, writing programs demands attention to detail. A single period out of place can create a "bug" that may take hours to trace. (pp. 69–70)

While newer authoring programs such as *HyperCard* or *ToolBook* are much easier to master than programming languages such as PASCAL or C, the developer still needs to learn a tremendous amount of technical material to fully develop any substantial application. Also, while not underestimating the importance of good textbook design, the CAC software developer must work with interface design in a medium for which few English faculty are trained and for which there is much less readily available help from publishers. Finally, in developing software, there is the central challenge of outlining concretely what one believes to happen when writers engage in the process of creating text.

Turning Knowledge into Software

At the heart of even the most ambitious computer program—whether it be a NASA navigational program or, closer to home,

John Smith's *Writing Environment* (WE)—there is the simplest on/off action of electronic current. This most essential fact of computer operations has a powerful influence on the writing of software and the way knowledge is embodied within programming code. This discussion offers a brief examination of the ways in which knowledge is classified and represented in software design, and of the implications that inform how software is written. Understanding this connection provides a context for this examination and helps explain why some approaches to composition are more likely than others to be computationally rendered.

There were, properly speaking, three progenitors of the modern digital computer. The idea of the computer was first conceived by Charles Babbage, venerable British mathematician and inventor, in 1833. His "analytical engine" was never built due to, what were then, insurmountable engineering problems (Johnson, 1987, p. 61). Just over one hundred years later, in 1936, English mathematician and logician Alan M. Turing (1937) set out to prove some esoteric results in symbolic logic and wrote one of the most innovative, yet little-known, documents of the twentieth century: "On Computable Numbers, with an Application to the *Entscheidungsproblem.*" In what Joseph Weizenbaum (1976) has called "one of the greatest triumphs of the human intellect," Turing laid out the theoretical foundation for all digital computers up to the present time, showing how to build one a full decade before his design would actually be realized in working form (p. 58). It was left to John Van Neumann to build the first computer and to set up its basic design configuration.

Like so many machines of our age, the computer does not convey physical power—it has almost no moving mechanical parts. The computer redefined the term machine to include those devices which are transformers of "information," usually through electronic impulse. The distributor of the modern automobile ignition system, a mechanical configuration of gears, a shaft, and cams, which timed the firing of spark plugs, has been largely replaced with the nonmechanical "control module" or "on-board computer," which consists of silicon chips controlling electronic impulses to the spark plugs as well as controlling a host of other functions. Those electronic impulses, traveling at the speed of light, represent and convey information.

The representation and processing of information in the form of electronic impulse is simply more difficult to do for some kinds of information, because it demands a descriptive precision that is not always so available. We can describe precisely, for example, the cognitive steps in determining the square root of a number, but who would purport to know precisely the steps that lead to a poem, a short story, or a freshman essay?

Procedural Knowledge

Weizenbaum (1976) asserts that if we understand a phenomenon in *all* its behavioral rules, we can express it in the form of a computer program. To understand and program a phenomenon, one must break it down into its smallest parts, or in the parlance of programming, its procedures. A set of procedures is called an algorithm. The set of procedures for finding out if a number is prime, for example, is pretty straightforward and might be mapped out like this:

1. Determine the number to be tested (computer user gives the information).
2. Call that number A.
3. Set the number to divide by, X, equal to 2.
4. Divide A by X.
5. If there is no remainder, go to step 8. Otherwise proceed to the next step.
6. Add 1 to X.
7. Is X now equal to A? If so, go to step 9; otherwise return to step 4 and repeat the loop.
8. Print "The number is not prime" and end.
9. Print "The number is prime" and end. (Johnson, 1987, p. 84)

The activity of finding prime numbers is logical and mathematical from the start. Writing a simple word-processing program is relatively easy, since text use has prescribed rules that the programmer can follow.

For phenomena which are not wholly or inherently rule-bound—the activity of writing, and much of life, for example—the task becomes much more difficult. If we were to attempt to write a program that could diagnose even a fairly limited problem, such as a car not starting, we would have a terrific challenge setting out the procedures involved. We would be facing what has become known as the "knowledge-acquisition bottleneck" (Johnson, 1987, p. 164). We could prioritize a list of problem-solving questions which the user could answer and for which she could write appropriate algorithms: "Is charge in battery 12 volts? If yes, proceed to the next question. Are the battery terminal leads securely fastened to the terminals? If no, tighten the leads. If yes, proceed to the next question" (and so on). But how do we program a mechanic's years of experience (e.g., "The points are always closing up on that year of VW Beetle") or intuition (e.g., "I'm not sure why, but this sounds like the fuel pump isn't working")?

Reducing expert behaviors to procedural steps has been the challenge for researchers who work with Intelligent Tutoring Systems (ITS), computer programs that teach students what experts do when confronted by a given problem. The answer to the problem has been "knowledge engineering." Martha Polson (Polson & Richardson, 1988) explains:

> A knowledge engineer interviews an expert and designs a computational representation for delivering the knowledge, usually a rule-based formalism. This implementation does not necessarily correspond to the way the human expert reasons, especially in novel, unfamiliar situations or when providing explanations . . . However, knowledge-engineering tools and techniques, that is, ways of extracting and codifying information, are becoming more and more useful for ITS development as attention is paid toward making representations more faithful to the breadth and depth of expert reasoning. (p. 4)

Knowledge engineers, through intensive interviews with many experts, attempt to identify the problem-solving strategies which those experts employ and which underlie other, more difficult-to-identify processes, such as intuition.

In the example just given—diagnosing an ignition problem

in an automobile— one might not be able to produce algorithms for intuitive knowledge, but the general task still lends itself to description in procedural terms. Similar tasks have been represented successfully in computational form at the Intelligent Systems Branch of the Air Force Human Resources Lab, where programs walk the user through the diagnosis for a broken-down tank or the process for changing the orbit of a satellite. In CAC programming, programs that analyze text for grammatical "correctness" are examples of such procedural programs. The speed and vast memory of the computer help to make up for its lack of experience or intuition.

Declarative Knowledge

Finding out whether a number is prime or checking on subject-verb agreement are considered types of "procedural knowledge." A second level of knowledge might be called "declarative knowledge," general knowledge about a particular area, for example, South American geography. The *Scholar* project, an early attempt to program information about South American geography, required an elaborate, semantic net representation of the knowledge base involved, one that consisted of various nodes which represented a wide range of concepts, such as countries, products, capitals, latitudes, forms of government, and so on (Carbonell, 1970, pp. 190–202). Programs in the area of declarative knowledge have tended to employ Socratic dialogue between the program and the user. The key to successful programming of declarative knowledge is to firmly establish the boundaries of that knowledge area and to keep the user within that domain. For example, in the area of CAC programming, *Confer* would be an example of such a program. The program interacts with the user in the analysis of a single short story, and it focuses entirely on text-based questions and responses— a highly defined knowledge base.

Qualitative Knowledge

In terms of computational representation, the ability to reduce information and procedures to mathematical representation—

the most challenging area for programmers and the one most relevant to composition studies—is "qualitative knowledge," the knowledge that allows us to operate in dynamic and changing environments. This is the knowledge base that allows us to process all of our knowledge to find the best ways to solve a problem or to create a piece of art such as a short story or essay. Sheldon Klein and his associates have attempted to write this type of program, an "automatic novel writer," which produces passages such as the following:

> The day was Monday. The pleasant weather was sunny. Lady Buxley was in a park. James ran into Lady Buxley. James talked with Lady Buxley. Lady Buxley flirted with James. James invited Lady Buxley. Lady Buxley was with James in a hotel. Lady Buxley was near James. James caressed Lady Buxley with passion. James was Lady Buxley's lover. Marion following them saw the affair. Marion was jealous. (Qtd. in Boden, 1977, p. 300)

This passage reveals the ability of a programmer like Klein to extract from a qualitative knowledge base some system of *procedural knowledge,* which in this case provides what might be a skeleton of a murder mystery, but not the knowledge base that underlies style and subtlety, and in the instance of a murder mystery, surprise. A complex activity like writing clearly draws upon procedural, declarative, and qualitative knowledge bases— how the mind "processes" that knowledge in the completion of the writing task is something about which we know very little. Intelligent Tutoring Systems (ITS) experts continue to work on the problem of representing all three knowledge bases and their interactions. Polson (Polson & Richardson, 1988) says that "one of the most challenging issues will be constructing a metatheory that unifies and shows the relationships between procedural, declarative, and qualitative knowledge" (p. 5). The need in programming for a clear mapping out of knowledge operations makes cognitive approaches to composition, with the highly defined cognitive models offered by researchers like Linda Flower and John Hayes, appealing to many who work in CAC programming. In fact, the best-funded and most technically ambitious CAC projects have been cognitive-based research projects.

The alliance of cognitive science and computers is not a new one. The close link between cognitive science and computer technology forms the basis for the work of composition cognitivists. In their landmark "Empirical Explorations of the Logic Theory Machine: A Case Study in Heuristics," Newell and Simon (Newell, Shaw, & Simon, 1957) made an assertion that is the basis for a cognitive approach to writing theory: "that programmed computer and human problem solver are both species belonging to the genus 'Information Processing System'" (Qtd. in Weizenbaum, 1976, p. 169). This is a profound declaration of equality between computer and human—one that elevates the computer, at least in its potentialities, and that abases humanity, so that Newell and Simon can even talk of our "programmability" (Weizenbaum, 1976, p. 169). While much vehement debate has occurred in the field of computer science over the validity of Newell and Simon's equating of human and machine, the comparison of the two in computer programming is hard to avoid. As Bolter (1984) points out:

> Man can solve problems in one way, machines in another. But in fact, the analogy remains firm in the minds of programmers. Computer programs are open to inspection, and human ways of thinking are not. When a programmer devises an algorithm for playing chess or for analyzing English grammar, he can hardly avoid regarding human performance by analogy with his invisible, intelligible algorithm. As one psychologist has put it, the computer model of the mind is the only working model available and even a bad model is better than none. (pp. 193–194)

In a sense, the strength and appeal of Newell and Simon's General Problem Solving (GPS) theory is its ability to schematize human thought (or its model) in a way that has eluded other theorists of cognitive activities. This has, in effect, put the onus on humans to think like computers, instead of forcing computers to think like humans.

As teachers of writing who use CAC programs, we need to be sensitive to this dynamic. For example, Smith's *WE* program, which will be discussed later in more detail, attempts to aid the student writer in all parts of the writing process (as Smith understands them)—*except* for the "social aspects of writing," as he puts it. Why the omission of that important, some might say key, area? It is the one area of his model that falls within the qualitative knowledge area—as we have seen, the most difficult to program for. The result of its exclusion from the program is that students using WE will not address those concerns, will be practicing a model of writing, and will presumably adopt that model at some cognitive level. The important question is to what degree does their thinking start to reflect the program and what it is able to do, rather than the inverse.

Computers are not flexible. That is, either one uses them and plays by their rules, or one does not use them. As we have seen, the computer is being widely adopted as a tool for writing. Anyone debating whether computers are good or bad for us is missing the point, for computers and CAC programs *are* here to stay and are quickly becoming universal in the classroom and workplace. New CAC programs are being released almost every day. This technology—the computer and the software we run on it—has the power to redefine not only *what* we consider text, but more importantly, *how* we mentally produce text. If the demands of binary language require knowledge to be reduced to precisely defined procedures and algorithms, and if that favors, and even in a sense validates, cognitive models of writing, and if the CAC programs that are most widely used are cognitively based, then our practice and our thinking about writing will follow suit. In that very important sense, computer-aided composition has the power to be a defining force in composition studies.

Chapter 3

The "Who" and "How" of CAC Software Development

To put it simply, much of my research was the gathering of stories. I grew up in a family of construction workers, and I have always loved the stories behind the building of edifices—houses, skyscrapers, dams, stone walls. My father was a stonemason, and he remembers all his walls—the one where he forgot an anchor stone and was called back, a year later, to pick up the washed out section of wall and rebuild it—the one where the customer was running out of money and insisted that my father complete the job by using oversize stone in the backcourses (my father still sees the bulges in the wall where those stones shifted and marred the lovely field-stone front of his wall). In each of those stories is a lesson about building stone walls, if one cares to listen closely and learn. Computer programs are edifices, too—edifices of the mind. This chapter describes the "who" and "how" of their construction—the builders and methods—and in these stories, there is much to learn, too.

Each account illustrates an approach for the design and development of CAC software. In that sense, the accounts provide and illustrate development models, and while there is certainly overlap between and exceptions to those suggested models, my review of the literature, my discussions with CAC specialists, and the interviews that form the heart of this study show the accounts to be reasonably typical descriptions of the primary approaches to current CAC software development. From the analysis of the data, five areas of concern emerged for structuring and illuminating the narrative accounts. They are as follows, and in the accounts they share the titles listed below:

1. *Getting Started/Origins and Models:* Identifies the roots of

the development effort, the inception of the program: seeing and reacting to other programs, attending a conference, wanting to program an exercise, responding to a research problem, or attempting to model certain writing behaviors. This discussion also attempts to identify models of the writing process or behavior, if any, on which the designer based her programming effort.

2. *Design and Development:* Describes the people involved in the development effort, how they worked together, and the way the program was designed. For example, if the project was a group effort, was responsibility divided up, or was the collaboration less structured? Did the designer also write the program code?

3. *User Input and Program Revision:* Examines the way user feedback is utilized during the development and revision stages of the development effort. This discussion also examines the way revision of the program takes place. Some of the issues covered include field testing, methods of evaluation, types of user feedback, and impediments to revision.

4. *Funding:* Examines the funding for the development effort. This discussion includes such areas as the benefits of for-profit software marketing, the role of defense-related funding, and the general lack of funding for some models of software development.

5. *Institutional Reward and Recognition:* Examines the response of academic institutions to the design efforts of faculty, especially in terms of acknowledgment, release time, and the treatment of CAC software in tenure and promotion deliberations.

Woven into this fabric are the idiosyncratic details of individual lives and the contexts that influenced the software. This chapter also provides insight into the people who are creating CAC programs. Each model description ends with a brief review of its most important characteristics.

Taken as a group, the four principal models for software development in this study offer a rich diversity of approaches and aims, a diversity not suggested by the scarcity of literature devoted to the subject of academic software development. In their general survey of institutional models for software development, Jack Chambers and Dorothy Ohl Lewis (1988) simply divide those development projects into sole designer and team design approaches (pp. 95–97). In fact, there is something like a continuum that reflects finer and more important differences between development approaches than a simple delineation based on the number of participants involved.

At one end of the continuum is what I term the *Lone Developer Model*. In this model, we find a writing teacher whose classroom experience suggests a need for a certain kind of program that does not seem available in the marketplace. With little access to funding, the teacher adopts a practical approach—she uses whatever equipment she has available to her and enlists the aid of any willing volunteer. She most likely tries out the program on her own students and makes changes based on what she sees them doing with it. If the program gets complicated, perhaps she hires a programmer. In terms of technical sophistication, the program is modest. Yet, it fills a niche, finds its way into the classroom immediately, and becomes, hopefully, a useful tool for that part of the writing process which it addresses. That is the best reward the designer is likely to receive, for these are the kinds of efforts that English departments prefer to lump in with general class preparation—with the nitty gritty of pedagogy. As such, little notice is likely to be taken of the program.

At the other end of the continuum is the *Research-Based Design Team*, a group of CAC researchers and specialists from various fields (education, psychology, possibly computer science) who work on programs that advance research interests. They work from highly defined and empirically based models of the writing process, and their programs are structured around those models. These programs are likely to make use of very sophisticated and expensive technology, and they require a great deal of funding. Thus, government agencies, defense-related concerns, and corporate sponsors are often part of the funding picture for these projects. Perhaps for that reason, or because of the competition for limited funding, the individuals interviewed for this model were reluctant to discuss exactly who is funding their work or the dollar amounts of their project budgets. It is clear, however, that those funding sources exert some influence on the development process and on the final program design. These are programs that may not make their way into most classrooms for many years, which is par for the course in this development model, given that the primary aim of the work is research oriented. It is their research focus that gives these projects their value within the institution. This work, as long as it results in publishable research, is viewed favorably in the reward structure of the university. In this model, CAC design weighs favorably in decisions about tenure and promotion.

Along the continuum, closer to the lone programmer end, we find the *Small Design Group Model*. In this model, one finds a small group of writing teachers, pooling their energies and talents, to produce software. Like the lone programmer, they are likely to base their program on their classroom experience and their observation of students; yet their program is likely to be more ambitious in its pedagogical goals and technical sophistication than those in the lone programmer model. The developers usually pursue funding at the institutional level or through lower-level grant programs (say $10,000 versus the $450,000 figure that a researcher like John Smith uses as an example of a project budget; J.B. Smith, 1989, interview). Much of this funding will be used to hire programmers. The work of these designers is likely to receive little reward or recognition from their departments and institutions, even if the program enjoys praise from others in the field.

Further along the continuum from the small design group is another group of academics, but in this scenario—the *Entrepreneurial Design Group Model*—the designers form a private company for the development and distribution of their software. These designers see themselves as CAC specialists, and as such, they are likely to have more technical expertise than their peers in the previous two models. For example, they are likely to do their own programming and to see that task as more enjoyable and valuable than do nonprogrammer-designers. Their combination of expertise, their power over their own work agenda, and the profits they derive from the sale of their software allow these designers more time for "playing" with program design and for revision of the program itself. Because their programming efforts exist outside the university, issues of departmental reward and recognition do not obtain.

Related to the entrepreneurial model and included in that discussion as a sort of subset is the *Professional Software Development Model*. In this model, software is developed for profit, but the designers are not academics. While they may have experience as teachers of writing, these designers are now full-time software developers and therefore must be more sensitive to the marketplace than the designers in the other models. That marketplace is likely to include the classroom as only part of a larger target group, usually the business sphere. Because they design for a business market that, in general, possesses more powerful hardware and larger pocketbooks than do writing programs, they can design more technically sophisticated and demanding programs than the developers who sell for the writing classroom.

Each approach is illustrated and explored through the accounts and comments of designers like Mimi Schwartz, Nancy Kaplan, Taylor, and Smith. Their stories help define the approaches, yet this is not to say that the experience of any one designer encompasses the experience of all other designers within the model. There is no logical reason, for example, why a designer in the lone programming model could not work with a more formal design protocol than Schwartz did. Yet, the accounts reveal a number of reasons why most designers in that model would not. In that sense, in the exploration of why the stones were placed in the way they were, if you will, the accounts are both illustrative and representative of each model.

The development models address the first two of the five areas of inquiry outlined in chapter 1: the who and how of current program design. Through the stories of the designers, one learns how CAC software tools are built, as well as the fundamental relationship of that process to their final shape. Before exploring the future direction of CAC software development, we must take this first step and find out where we are today.

The Lone Developer Model

This model for program development is closest to the one John Kemeny and the developers of BASIC imagined in 1958, a model in which classroom teachers would have the skills and resources to create their own computer programs. James Strickland's 1981 program, *FREE*, is an example of such an effort in CAC programming. Strickland was inspired by the model of writing in Peter Elbow's *Writing without Teachers* (1973) and knew that no CAC program existed which reflected the pedagogy suggested in Elbow's book. Strickland wrote his freewriting program in BASIC on an Apple microcomputer with 48k memory.

My research suggests that Strickland's example is now an exception in the field of CAC development, for two important reasons. One is the development of higher-level programming languages which more easily meet the complex programming demands of increasingly sophisticated CAC programs, but which are often beyond the ken of classroom writing teachers. These languages, such as Turbo Pascal, C, and a new generation of object-oriented program languages such as C++, often mean enlisting the aid of a hired programmer. BASIC has been rewritten in an attempt to meet more sophisticated needs, but none of the program developers I spoke with now uses BASIC. The second reason, as just suggested, is the increasing sophistication of CAC programs. When Strickland was asked for a copy of *FREE*, he hesitated and expressed embarrassment at what he called its "primitiveness" (Strickland, 1988, interview). He pointed out that "any word processing program can now do what I was trying to do with *FREE*." By way of contrast, a recently developed program like Dan Burns's *Thoughtline* requires substantial computer memory, processing speed, and hard drive space. Also, it was written in LISP, a programming language designed for artificial intelligence programs. Programs like *Thoughtline* require not only more technological knowledge on the part of the designer, but also a great deal more development time, as much as three to four years (Selfe, 1989a, interview), as well as technological resources. As Selfe argues, "These are beyond the reach of the everyday classroom teacher." Mimi Schwartz's experience in the development of *Prewrite* is perhaps a more accurate representation of the "lone" programming model as it exists today.

Mimi Schwartz is an associate professor and director of the writing program at Stockton State College in New Jersey. Schwartz, possessing the energy of her native New York City, engages in a wide range of professional activities. She teaches a variety of writing courses, has authored the texts *Writing for Many Roles* (1985) and *Writers' Craft, Teachers' Art* (1991), a forthcoming memoir entitled *Swimming above the Black Line*, a guide to writing college entrance essays, and, at present, is completing a novel. She seems to possess a natural inquisitiveness. As a result, the impetus to create a software program was, for her, a mix of curiosity, challenge, and a nose for the market niche. She recalls:

> I guess the software program . . . I just sort of had an idea. I've done a number of these kinds of things. I wrote a booklet, *How to Write Your College Application Essay*, that did very well. I'm still getting good royalties from that. So I was thinking, the software thing intrigued me, so I decided to see what I could do with that. (M. Schwartz, 1989, interview)

The inspiration for the actual program, according to Schwartz, came from seeing a presentation by Hugh Burns and from a desire to humanize the prewriting programs then available. She says:

> I [wanted] to write a program that was very uncomputerese. That was the challenge. I didn't like all the jargon that was built into some of the early prewrite programs. (M. Schwartz, ibid)

Schwartz set out to design a prewriting program that would "get things out on the page, to look and see what's there that looks interesting."

She claims that the program was not based on a formal model of the writing process; however, the structure of the program corresponds closely with her later description of how she believes writing takes place:

> Writing is, well, the aim is to try to get a lot of stuff out, to see what's there that looks interesting, and build from that. The process of building is, well, you build and you expand out, and then you come back, and it's much more of a holistic process. (M. Schwartz, ibid)

Interestingly, the structure of the program follows three cycles of expansion and compression which are similar to her description of the writing process quoted in the passage above. Following is one such cycle from the program:

> One way to find a topic is by freewriting. Just type in the first five ideas that come to mind and don't think about whether they're good or not. Try it! Okay. Are you interested in writing about any of these ideas? (A "Yes" answer produces "Which one?" A "No" answer sends you back to freewriting or allows you to exit the program.)

> Think about a working title for your piece (less than one line).

When you've moved through this cycle from freewriting to title, you begin the next cycle with another expansive question—"Why did you choose to write about _____? (Answer as fully as you can)"—and the cycle is repeated. Even though Schwartz asserts that the program was not based on a formal model, the "building out and coming back" she describes as taking place in the writing process are indeed reflected in the structure of *Prewrite*. It is interesting to note that Schwartz seemed at first unaware that the structure of her program should so closely parallel her own model of the writing process. She sees the program as a more unstructured and creative way to "get over the blank page," yet an analysis of the program reveals it to be highly structured, and her interview comments suggest that her sense of the writing process acted as at least a subconscious model in the design of the program.

The complexity of the programming effort dictated that Schwartz, unlike Strickland before her, could not work alone. Indeed, my research turned up very few examples of teachers truly working alone in the development of a CAC program. While Schwartz is solely responsible for the design of the program, she collaborated with a series of programmers to create its actual working substantiation. Working with her high-school-age son, Alan, who could program in BASIC, Schwartz developed a prototype of *Prewrite* that she used in the computer writing lab at Stockton State, receiving positive student response. Realizing that developing a final version of the program was beyond her son's abilities, she hired a programmer. Even though *Prewrite* is a relatively unsophisticated program in terms of its structure—it is a straightforward prewriting heuristic that prompts for user response, but does nothing with those responses beyond printing them—the programmer whom Schwartz hired to rework the prototype version, written in BASIC, rewrote the program in a higher-level language.

While Schwartz did not explain, in her interview, why the programmer used a higher-level language, there are a number of rationales for doing so. Such a rewrite may have offered the programmer more modularized code, making subsequent revisions easier. He may have rewritten the code to make it more economical in size, reducing its memory requirements and making it attractive to more of the "low-end" users, those with less powerful machines. One of the positive results of rewriting *Prewrite* was that the program could then allow teacher-users to customize and monitor the program itself.

The difference between Strickland's experience, doing his own programming, and Schwartz's, working with a programmer, might seem rather insignificant, but in fact, the collaboration of program designer and programmer is one that can directly affect the final design of the program and even compromise the designer's original aims. Schwartz recalls working with her programmer:

> I put an ad in the paper for a programmer. I was looking for someone who was not into computerese, so I hired someone who was a programmer, but had a Ph.D. in psychology. I figured he would be humanistic. Which was wrong. The battle was always that I kept on saying I wanted it [*Prewrite*] to be a program that people who knew nothing about computers could use. And programmers just don't think that way. His problem with me was that I had absolutely no idea how programming worked, so I had no

idea what things were easy for him to do and what things were hard. (M. Schwartz, ibid)

For example, Schwartz remembers her negotiations with the programmer over the initial user sign-on. In keeping with her desire for a more humane voice in the program, she wanted the program to say, "Hi! What's your name?" The programmer needed to have the full name with a verification (i.e., "Your name is John Doe. Is that correct? [Y/N"]). His argument was that, without verification, the user might have a typo in her name and would be unable to recall her file in future work sessions. In addition, according to Schwartz, the programmer saw the language of the verification request as appropriate for the discourse of computers: "He couldn't see that this discourse wasn't appealing to people who didn't buy into it," she asserts. Schwartz's argument had to do with her theory of writing:

> In my writing process . . . the thing that I realized is that all my writing begins with a voice. So that if I can't get the voice right, I can't write it. So, that initial confrontations over the opening screens were very important to me, because I couldn't see the rest of it coming out. (M. Schwartz, ibid)

The final result was a compromise in *Prewrite's* opening, with the humane voice Schwartz demanded, followed by a slightly more computerized voice asking for the verification the programmer needed:

> Hi! What's your full name?
> Your name is _____ Is this correct? (Y/N)

The program then goes on to address the user by his or her first name. A sense of disjointedness seems to result from the informality of the enthusiastic "Hi!" followed by the formality of a request for a full name which is then repeated back to the user. The verification could have taken place during a later save function and not impinged upon the opening of the program. This is a case where the designer's aims were needlessly compromised by a programmer's strict adherence to what he felt was good programming practice, putting his criteria for the program ahead of the designer's.

Recalling her work with a hired programmer during the development of *Wordswork* (formerly *Wordsworth II*), Cynthia Selfe echoes Schwartz's experience. Like Schwartz, she had to negotiate with her programmer:

> I finally said, "Hey, look! You're making the technology constrain the writer. You have to settle for some of these things [design characteristics the programmer disagreed with]." It was a process of negotiation. So it was really frustrating when we were in it, but in retrospect, it was almost funny. I know that we learned things through the experience of coding. (Selfe, 1989a, interview)

The gap between a designer's original vision of a program and its final shape may be unnecessarily widened when the designer lacks programming experience. As Helen Schwartz, creator of the award-winning CAC program *SEEN*, says of her experience with a hired programmer, "I was not in a position to evaluate his work. For example, choosing what language to program in. I had no way of knowing if that decision was correct or not" (H. Schwartz, 1992, interview). This situation leaves a great deal of power in the hands of the non-content expert collaborator. Selfe agrees, and she suggests that designers should know at least some programming, even if they are not going to write their own code. Having had some PASCAL, she recalls, "I was at least able, when the programmer had a failing of imagination, to say, 'Yes, you can do it!' But I was not able to direct or guide" (Selfe, 1989a, interview). Her sentiments were echoed by many of the program developers I interviewed; but even Helen Schwartz, who had a good working knowledge of BASIC, finally concluded about working with hired programmers: "I never want to do it again."

Fred Kemp argues for a return to program designers who also write their own code. He believes that the act of actually writing the code for a program generates new ideas for the design of that program and allows for quick and easy revisions:

> There is something in the actual process of writing the program that acts as an invention heuristic itself. It generates ideas, it generates paths for you to take, which when filtered through your professional training in composition and rhet-

oric, can generate new ways of handling a program that a nonprogrammer just wouldn't discover. (Kemp, 1989, interview)

The combination of programming expertise and the classroom teacher's immediate access to classroom use and observation quickens the design-revision cycle. As Kemp notes:

The second thing is that the teacher-programmer can observe the programs in action, and when something happens in the program, whether it's an interface screen situation or some part of the central mechanism of the program, the teacher is sitting there evaluating it in terms of pedagogy and instructional approach... When I see things happen on the screen, in my mind I'm thinking "program lines," and this, I think, is important. (Kemp, ibid)

Without having to negotiate program revisions or having to follow more structured design protocols, the teacher-programmer can substantially reduce the time lag between user input and revision: "The next class comes in and you've already dumped the program—the revision—in" (Kemp, ibid).

Unfortunately, the faculty member who decides to design and develop a CAC program will most likely work with a programmer-collaborator, despite the limitations of such an approach. The complexity of higher-level programming languages and the time it takes to become expert in their use make the training time prohibitive for practicing classroom teachers or imposing to newcomers. The demands of writing, compiling, and debugging thousands of lines of complicated program code are likely to keep the number of practitioner-programmers small.

On the other hand, new hypertext and hypermedia authoring systems like *HyperCard* and *ToolBook*, which are based on object-oriented programming languages, allow even nonprogrammers to create highly sophisticated software programs. These programs have the potential to revive the lone faculty-developed software program, at least from a technical perspective (see chapter 4).

Schwartz completed a "rough" version of *Prewrite* and made changes in the program on the basis of user response, specifically the input of high school teachers who were using the program in their writing courses. That input, combined with the informal observation of her own students in the Stockton State computer writing lab, led to the removal of a number of the program's audience-based questions. Schwartz did no formal testing of the program. This use of user input and informal observation for program revisions was the common method of testing programs in three of the four design models suggested by my research. Only the large design teams, following highly structured development protocols, did formal testing of programs during the development process; the other subjects cited a lack of necessary staff and funding.

Soon after completing *Prewrite*, Schwartz entered into discussions with CONDUIT, the software marketing consortium. They requested a number of revisions in the program that included new functions and would require substantial amounts of programming. Schwartz broke off those discussions, refusing to conduct such a complete reworking of the program. She comments, "It's not like someone asking you to rewrite a piece of writing. For that, you can sit down and do it. With software, you need to find a programmer and begin the process again. It's a much bigger... it's a different psychological thing" (H. Schwartz, 1992, interview). Later, when her eventual software publisher, MindScape, saw a potential elementary school market for *Prewrite*, Schwartz did revise the program. In this case, revising the software meant merely changing and decreasing the number of prompts. The former activity was built into the original program and required no real reprogramming.

Schwartz received no outside funding for the development of *Prewrite*. She paid her son two hundred dollars for his programming work in the development of the prototype; the informal sales of the prototype paid for the programmer she eventually hired to write the final version of the program. Since the program was written on an Apple and was designed for the Apple microcomputers in her computer lab, the hardware resources Schwartz needed were readily available. In terms of funding and resources, this model for program development falls at the least expensive end of the design and development continuum, the sphere characterized by the least amount of institutional support and recognition for such efforts. Aside from watching her students use the program in the lab, all the development was done off campus, without the aid of college computing resources. While she enjoyed recognition for her instrumental role in acquiring the first computer writing lab in New Jersey, she received no formal recognition for her software work from either her department or her college.

However, Schwartz would not overemphasize the value of the program or even of computers in general. Of all those interviewed, she was the least enthusiastic about technology and the least willing to acknowledge its deeper noetic implications:

> It's a useful tool ... There are certain people that definitely, you know, people who have spelling, handwriting problems, writer's block—I will push them more toward the computer. It's like a good typewriter; it's a good tool. I'm not hooked on it as anything more than a convenient technology. (H. Schwartz, 1992, interview)

Indeed, Schwartz would have done no more work in software development regardless of institutional reward: "I think it can help people, and there are certain people it can help a lot, but I don't think it's worth the extra pedagogy to do this." In this sense only, Schwartz's experience is not typical of other single-person program designers. While most others using this approach attempted no more in the way of new program design, they all remained committed to using technology and convinced of its significant impact on composition theory and pedagogy.

What can be termed the defining characteristics of the lone program developer model? First, the effort is seldom, if rarely, the work of a single practitioner/programmer. It is more likely to be a partnership between an expert, usually the writing teacher who is also a computer enthusiast, and a programmer. This collaboration seems to require lengthy negotiation and may ultimately constrain some of the creativity in design concepts. Program development in this model is informal. The idea for the program is likely to come out of classroom practices and needs, perhaps the desire to computerize a favorite pedagogy, as in the case of Strickland's *FREE* and Schwartz's *Prewrite*. Revisions of the program are more likely to be based on user feedback and informal observation of its use than formal site testing. In part, this may be a result of the inadequate funding these efforts are likely to receive, as well as the general informality of the development model. Because these programs are designed for existing classroom technology (for example, microcomputers like the Apple IIe, instead of expensive Sun terminals common to engineering departments) technological resources tend to be readily available. The expense of a programmer, a relatively modest one given the type of programs developed in this model, is the greatest cost in the development effort. My research suggests that there is little institutional support for these kinds of programming efforts.

The Small Design Group Model

Moving up the continuum, the next model suggested by my research is what might be termed the small design group. The small design group is usually a collaboration between two or three practitioners and often a hired programmer, though one of the designers may also know some programming. There are numerous examples of such small design group programs: Valerie Arms and Jim Gibson's *Create/Recreate,* Ray and Dawn Rodrigues's *Creative Problem-Solving,* Donald Ross and Robert Rasche's *Eyeball,* Helen Schwartz and Louis Nachman's *Organize,* and Cynthia Selfe and Billie Wahlstrom's *Wordswork.* Of the programs included in this study, the development of *Prose* is a good example of this design model. It was the creation of Nancy Kaplan, Stuart Davis, and Joseph Martin, all lecturers in the writing program at Cornell University at the time of the program's creation.

The design and development of *Prose,* a program designed to facilitate instructor feedback on student texts, followed a much more formal track than did *Prewrite.* The original idea developed out of classroom practice, specifically the observation of instructor feedback on student texts and a desire to improve the quality of that feedback. Kaplan recalls:

> Part of my interest in the project, to begin with, was not so much how it was going to have an immediate impact

> on students' writing behavior or their sense of their own autonomy and authority over their texts, because I've always known that instructors are far too intrusive in their students' work and that students are far too docile in that process . . . In my particular position, you see all kinds of horrors when you mark student papers; and it [the program] seems like a way—a fairly nonthreatening way—of handing instructors a new mechanism for doing their work that will encourage them to think about that work in new and different ways. (N. Kaplan, 1989, interview)

To effect such an impact on instructors, the design team envisioned a hypertextual program that would allow nonsequential creation of instructor comments through flagging and windowing, as well as layered handbook and workbook screens for mechanical errors.

The program has a twofold goal. It offers instructors mechanisms for giving useful feedback on student papers—modeling, in effect, the designers' sense of what feedback should look like. The way that feedback is presented to students offers them an alternative model of revision from the one the designers believed they saw in the classroom. Kaplan describes students' poor revision behavior:

> What I used to see, or thought I used to see, was a student who looked at the piece of paper on which his text and my responses were written, and who then went to whatever was closest to the top and made a change, and then moved on and worked from the top down, word by word. You saw a lot of tinkering at the word and phrase levels, and almost no conception of revision in any domain other than the word or phrase. (N. Kaplan, ibid)

The model that underlies *Prose* provides a global view of the text, first, and a prescribed order of revisions that may only address word- and phrase-level changes, last. Kaplan describes this model in terms of the program:

> To us it seems really important that the summary comment [the overall commentary that instructors typically append to the end of a student essay] actually sort of lay out the whole project [the revision of the student paper] as we envision it. But I also use the work-order feature to help

> students get a sense of the priorities, partly by making a very clear distinction for my students between comments and "please revise" remarks, and occasionally by setting a work order to first take a student some place other than the head of the document. (N. Kaplan, ibid)

The design of *Prose* is built on this model, which the designers hoped students would adopt as a more effective approach to revision.

A program of this sophistication requires a great deal of programming and revision, which requires funding. Therefore, before the development of the program could proceed very far, the group was faced with writing a funding proposal. A funding proposal requires, early on, a clear articulation of design goals. If the design of a program can be likened to the creation of written text, then these "writers" had to consider audience (members of the grant committee) needs early in the design process; they could not proceed very far into the development of the program by just "playing" with the design, at least in its broad parameters and stated goals.

Once the proposal for *Prose* was accepted, the development process started in earnest. The collaboration of Kaplan, Martin, and Davis was unstructured; that is, each member had input into all the important design decisions, and the group worked toward some form of consensus. Kaplan says:

> We worked pretty well together. Yes, I would have to say that, overall, it was smooth, and we did a lot of talking through of the design issues. I mean, we always talked about this stuff anyway, so in a sense, the collaboration wasn't new. But there were some difficult moments—actually, some really bad moments. But those usually occurred when we were feeling some deadline pressure, some pressure to produce. Then things got pretty heated; for example, when we were trying to finish up the documentation before sending the program off to Kinko's. (N. Kaplan, ibid)

While Kaplan characterizes the collaboration as "smooth," her interview response suggests the difficulties that can come with collaboration among equals. Helen Schwartz speaks to this issue in recalling her collaboration with Jack Nachman, *Organize:* "It's a problem. We were two colleagues working together, so I couldn't prod him, and he couldn't prod me. If you have unequal passion for a project, it's a problem" (H. Schwartz, 1992, interview). Kaplan said about the *Prose* project, "We don't talk about it anymore. We're still friends and we want to keep it that way!" (N. Kaplan, ibid)

For most writing teachers who want to create software, the development effort takes place outside of their salaried institutional work. The long hours and necessary meetings must then impinge upon their personal lives, and that can create stress both within the group and within their individual spheres:

> I'm a single parent, but neither of my two collaborators have any children. So, there were times when we were working on something, and I just had to up and leave because I had to pick up kids from daycare, or just go home and cook a meal, or whatever it might have been. (N. Kaplan, 1991b, interview)

While much collaboration within the group took place around the coffeepot in the writing workshop conference room, or in the suite of offices the three colleagues shared, there were also many 10 p.m. meetings after Kaplan's four- and seven-year-old daughters, Erica and Eva, were tucked into bed. She remembers, "Oh, 10 p.m. to 2 a.m. were prime-time *Prose* work hours." The two children, who once earned a dollar an hour to repeat the same combination of keystrokes on the computer until a hard-to-track-down bug occurred, expressed considerable resentment at the time Kaplan had to spend working on *Prose*. Kaplan now suggests that software development, when it takes place outside of professional duties, is almost impossible for anyone acting as a primary parent.

While the development effort was informal, by the later stages of the project, the individual strengths of the group members emerged. Each of the designers started taking responsibility for specific areas of the work:

> I did most of the program debugging, mostly because I had more patience, and I turned out to be better at it. So I did most of the negotiating with the programmers. Meanwhile, someone else would take over writing the documentation. (N. Kaplan, 1989, interview)

Because none of the three designers was an expert programmer, the group hired five student programmers during the course of the program's development and wrote none of the actual code themselves. But because the designers had some programming experience, when they had to negotiate design decisions with their programmers, they could do so with a sense of what was possible and reasonable, similar to the experience Selfe described earlier. Kaplan argues that hiring a programmer may mean losing the heuristic value of writing code, but this gives the designers substantially more time to work on other project concerns, such as writing documentation, negotiating with distributors, revising the program, and so forth (N. Kaplan, ibid).

As in the case of *Prewrite*, the primary mechanism for evaluating the program's design was informal observation of students who were using the program. For example, Kaplan observed many students who used *Prose* to read their instructor's revision comments, but who then moved to another word processor to actually rewrite the document. Moving out of the program often meant circumventing the guided revision effected by the instructor through the program's "work order" function. (This function forces students to make textual changes in a prescribed order.) Kaplan blames this phenomenon—of students leaving the program to make their actual revisions—on a technical constraint which the developers had to accept:

> Well, part of the reason for that is one of the disabilities of *Prose*—and it's something we are absolutely, at least for now, stuck with—namely, that you can't do face and font changes, that you lose a lot of formatting. In a well-designed computer environment, that wouldn't be . . . Now when we started this project, Apple kept promising a different core editor. The editor we're using comes supplied with the machine, so to speak. And it's pretty good—by IBM standards it's a "wowser"—but it's not good enough, because we're spoiled by face and font changes, and ruler changes, and other things. And they kept promising us that they were going to replace the thing at the heart of it, which is called "text edit," with something else called "core edit," which would allow us what is called a "rich-text format." But it never happened, and they abandoned it. So we were pretty well stuck with what we had. (N. Kaplan, ibid)

This is a good example of the way a technological limitation can impair program design and encourage some users to ignore one of a program's central functions. Kaplan believes the work-order function effectively forces the student to follow and thus learn effective revision strategies. Kaplan's conclusion—that the program's poor editor is driving the switch from *Prose* to another word processor during the actual revisions—reveals the way a technological factor can have a very real impact on program design and effectiveness.

While there was little the designers could do to rectify the problem, other problems they observed were addressed during program revisions. Throughout the program's three versions, revisions in design were often substantial, with a major overhaul of the file structure occurring between the second and third versions. The goal of these revisions was to give instructors and students more flexibility in the program, allowing students, for example, a "skip" function that allows them to skip over an instructor's "Please Revise" and "Comments" messages. As in the case of *Prewrite*, the revisions were largely based on user feedback and the informal observation of student users in the university writing program. As far as evaluating the program's success in meeting its main design goals, no formal testing was performed:

> Nobody's had the time to actually look at how instructors use it and whether their practice—using this kind of tool to respond to student grading—differs from their practice when they're using other tools, other ways of representing their work. (N. Kaplan, ibid)

In fact, not only has testing not occurred, but there are no current plans for future revisions to the program. *Prose* is now in the hands of McGraw-Hill, who is marketing it, but who has not implemented any program revisions.

A lack of formal funding is the primary reason for the lack of formal field testing and revision that the program now needs. The proposal for *Prose* was one of three computer project proposals the group submitted to Cornell University's College of Arts and Sciences and the one which was selected for funding. Additional funding came from an anonymous donor, from the

Cornell writing program, and from Apple Computer, Inc. While the program was funded, it was, for a program of this complexity, only adequately so. Kaplan points out: "We [received] from the institution a total of about $10,000 over three years, which . . . hardly [constitutes] massive support for a project of this sort" (N. Kaplan, ibid).

While the funding saw the designers through the three-year development period and its three successive versions of the program, the designers had to compromise the design of the program, due largely to a lack of additional funding. To illustrate, Kaplan explains that in the original design, the preprogrammed examples could be changed by any given instructor:

> That was something which we had designed to be flexible when we first wrote the design script for it. We weren't sophisticated enough at that stage to know that you were supposed to write out specifications for [quadrules] and things. So we actually wrote it out, but with the time and money available, it just didn't happen. (N. Kaplan, ibid)

The implication of that limitation for the program, according to Kaplan, is that the examples become stale for the student users and might not translate well into other learning environments at Cornell (N. Kaplan, ibid). However, the project budget simply did not allow for changes to the program's examples.

Kaplan explains that the group's reluctance to do any further work with *Prose* stems not only from the rigors of the task ("It's really the hardest work I've ever done"), but largely from the lack of institutional support from Cornell. She points to the meager funding for the project, and to the university's lack of interest in the group's work. In terms of the encouragement the group did receive, the following excerpt is illuminating:

> *Kaplan:* Occasionally, someone said a nice word or two.
> *LeBlanc:* How about in terms of recognition since then?
> *Kaplan:* None. No release time. The three of us did this in addition to our full-time jobs [as lecturers in the writing program]. The only thing we got formally from the university was acknowledgment that the thing itself [*Prose*] belonged to us, so that if we could market it, we'd get the money. There's been an award [1987 NCRIPTAL/

> EDUCOM Distinguished Software Award]. That wasn't even announced... frankly, the writing program has invested very little in computer-aided instruction. It has no demonstrable interest. (N. Kaplan, ibid)

It is interesting to note that even the Writing Project, which operates separately from Cornell's English department, failed to appreciate the importance of the group's work. That recognition has come from elsewhere, most notably in the NCRIPTAL/EDUCOM award the program earned in 1987.

To review, the small group model of CAC program development is a common one, accounting for 35 percent of the programs listed in Ellen McDaniel's 1987 bibliography of CAC software. The groups normally include two to four designers, usually working with one or more programmers. The cost of programming normally demands the pursuit of outside funding, often through the home institution, as in the case of *Prose*. While inspiration for such programs might come from the classroom-based experience of the practitioner-designers, the requisites of proposal writing and group collaboration demand a highly articulated set of goals early in the development process, allowing for less of the "play" described by program developers in two of the four models under study.

Because the program designers are writing teachers, first, and program designers, second, the development of a program, despite its rigors, must take place after the demands of a full teaching schedule. Indeed, 60 percent of the faculty program developers responding to EDUCOM's Academic Software Development Survey cite the lack of release time as the greatest barrier to program development (Keane & Gaither, 1988, p. 56). Mirroring Kaplan's experience, Keane and Gaither report that "faculty members expending considerable effort were not sure that administrators appreciated the importance of their work in software development" (p. 56).

This lack of support, both in terms of time and money, has design implications for this development model. It might mean not being able to make improvements in program design, or it might mean a lack of formal testing. In the case of *Prose*, it certainly means that desired improvements will not be made and that the pedagogical effectiveness of the program may be impaired.

The Entrepreneurial Design Group

"Entrepreneurial design," a term used by Chambers and Lewis to describe the efforts of the single faculty programmer, is an increasingly rare approach to software design. It is used here, more aptly, to describe program design teams that operate as private, profit-making companies. The Daedalus Group, producer of both *Mindwriter* and *Interchange,* is one such company, highly respected by those in the CAC field, and useful for illustrating this approach to software development. Paul Taylor, Locke Carter, Wayne Butler, and Fred Kemp are members of this group. Hugh Burns and Jim Parlett both act in an advisory capacity to the group, with the former holding the title of chairman of the board.

Interchange is a real-time conversation program designed for use on a standard file-transfer microcomputer network to create on-line classroom discussion. Unlike asynchronous systems such as bulletin boards or electronic mail, *Interchange* allows a group of users to be on-line at the same time and to converse on screen while displaying everyone's contributions. The program has five main components:

1. The individual student writes on a "scratch pad," and when ready, can send the comment into the main display window on the screen of every participant signed-on to the conference.

2. Comments appear on the main window as they arrive in chronological order, and the screen scrolls to make room for new incoming comments. Students can move through the text to reread what has been sent. In the latest version of the program, a hypertext component has been added which allows students the option of placing their new comments anywhere in the ongoing discussion, allowing for the elaboration of dialogues within the framework of the overall conversation.

3. Users can break off from the main conference and create subconferences to pursue new topics or lines of conversation.
4. The program has a split-screen capability that allows a conversation to take place in one window while the text under discussion appears on another.
5. The program can provide a hard-copy transcript of the conversation at the close of the session.

The hypertextual component of the software allows strings of responses to be reconstructed from the overall conversation. Participants might, for example, ask for all the responses that included a given word or phrase.

The program was developed in the windowless basement offices of the English department's Computer Research Lab at the University of Texas at Austin. On one side of the hall leading to the lab was a networked classroom of IBM PCs, and on the other side was the lab office, a messy and disorganized place full of computers in various states of repair, piles of programming manuals, errant floppy disks, and the constant flicker of computer screens—in short, a computer hacker's playground. Yet the hackers in this case were not computer scientists or engineering students. They were a group of English graduate students who, in 1984, took over the then new facility because no regular English faculty member knew what to do with it. In little time, this group of graduate students and self-taught programmers began to produce high-quality software that would eventually be integrated into something called the *Daedalus Instructional System*, which would win a 1990 NCRIPTAL/EDUCOM Award for Outstanding Software.

The leader of that group was Fred Kemp, now an assistant professor of English at Texas Tech University. In 1984, after years of teaching in the secondary schools, he went to the University of Texas to complete a doctorate in literary studies. In the summer of 1983, Kemp and his wife had sold their house, preparing to move to Austin and begin his studies. With part of the proceeds from the sale of their home, he purchased a TRS Model 4. With little to do that summer, Kemp taught himself how to program in BASIC. During his second semester in the program, Kemp heard that two faculty members had received a grant for new IBM computers but had then accepted teaching positions elsewhere. With no one capable of assembling the soon-to-arrive computers, Kemp volunteered, and Jerome Bump, then head of the English department and responsible administratively for the facility, promptly named Kemp—who had never used an IBM—assistant director of the lab.

Kemp readily admits that his initial interest had more to do with idle curiosity than vision:

> Jerry didn't know anything about computers, and he kind of wanted to play with them. That was my motivation—to play. None of us really expected much to come out of this; we were just trying to see what we could come up with. Jerry, because he was interested in the computers, encouraged that exploration. (Kemp, 1991, interview)

Kemp soon saw the pedagogical potential of the computers, and though he received little initial support for his ideas ("Even Jerry said I was a little crazy at first," he notes), Kemp had one very important predecessor at the university, someone whose work would prove influential and supportive. Hugh Burns, an Air Force officer who completed a doctorate in education at the university some five years before, had used as a germinal part of his dissertation research a computer-based invention program based on Aristotle's *topoi*, Burke's pentad, and the tagmemics of Young, Becker, and Pike. James Kinneavy, one of Kemp's professors and a member of Burns's original dissertation committee, alerted Kemp to Burns's work. Kemp remembers:

> I got that dissertation and started looking at it, and it was the first time I realized that anything that small had ever been done about computers. That was in the summer of 1984, and I decided then that we could take Hugh's programs—*TOPOI* and *TAGI*—off the mainframe and put them onto a PC and run a study on them. (Kemp, ibid)

Bump gave the project validity by dubbing it "Project Invention Heuristics" and left Kemp to program all day. Kemp was unhappy with the work of the computer science students who were hired to assist him, so he spent hours by himself, working with his self-taught skills in BASIC, to make the original memory-intensive program operate on a simple PC.

His efforts culminated in the event that moved him away for good from literary studies and into computer-based rhetoric: his delivery of a paper at the 1986 Conference on College Composition and Communication. Actually, Bump had written a paper on his and Kemp's initial studies with the program they had entitled *Idealog* (later to become *Mindwriter*), but he was unable to attend the conference and asked Kemp to deliver the paper instead. Kemp is a big man physically. He is known to speak up and at length on the subject of computers and writing; yet, this was his first paper and he was, in his own words, "terrified." Adding to his state of anxiety was the fear that Burns might be in the audience and might object to some of the criticisms Kemp had of Burns's original program. He recalls that presentation:

> This was the first session at the 4Cs, and everybody kept telling me, "You'll be lucky to get five people." We had about 120 in there. People were standing along the back wall and outside into the hall, and I was scared to death. You couldn't miss this tall guy in the back of the room in a blue Air Force uniform. My wife Jan, the night before, found the 4Cs' letter and the part where they said they don't like papers read. So I had stayed up all night memorizing the thing.... When I delivered the paper, it appeared that all these beautiful sentences were coming off the top of my head without my ever looking at the pages. It went very well, and afterwards Hugh came up and really congratulated me. We talked for about thirty minutes, and he offered to be on my committee, and at that point—if we are going to talk about an epiphany—I realized this was important stuff, and I could participate as a colleague in this venture. (Kemp, 1989, interview)

Kemp was the right person to undergo this conversion, for his personality and expertise helped draw other talented graduate students to the lab; not long after his CCCC paper, Paul Taylor, Wayne Butler, and Locke Carter joined the staff.

The formation of that original group was more propinquity than process. At a regional conference in Corpus Christi, Kemp and Taylor ran into other University of Texas graduate students, including Butler and Valerie Balister. The latter pair had been doing research and presenting papers on social constructivist theory, and at dinner, as Butler puts it, "theory met computers" (Butler, 1991, interview). Butler recalls:

> It was kind of funny. The Computer Research Lab at that time had Fred and Paul and thirty or forty computers—and no students. It was at that dinner that we said, "Well, let's see if we can turn it [the Computer Research Lab] into a classroom!" The next summer we started bringing students over. It wasn't an official thing—students didn't know the course was computer assisted when they signed up for it. We just sort of embarked on our own initiatives to do this team-teaching, collaborative learning, in the network's classroom environment. (Butler, ibid)

The strong connection between theory and software design, begun at a happenstance dinner, continues to characterize the development efforts of the group. In the case of *Interchange*, Butler's work in social constructivist theory would play a key role in the development of the program.

Paul Taylor is actually the principal developer of *Interchange*, though as typical of development in the Daedalus Group, many of its members would influence the final shape of the program. Taylor, recently hired as an assistant professor of English at Texas A&M University, is in many ways Kemp's opposite. Where Kemp is large and friendly, Taylor is almost ascetic in appearance; where Kemp is familiar and outgoing, Taylor is rather shy and softspoken; and where Kemp enjoys all levels of the Daedalus Group's work, the design, the marketing, the research and conference papers, Taylor's first love is the solitude and exactitude of writing program code. Indeed, in the last pursuit he is probably the best programmer of the group. For example, the inspiration for *Interchange* came from an academic conference, the 1987 Conference on College Composition and Communication, where Fred Kemp saw a demonstration of a rudimentary real-time conversation program designed by Trent Batson at Gallaudet University. Kemp returned to Austin and described what he saw; Taylor made it happen.

At the time, the Daedalus Group had not formally come into

being, though all its future members were working together in the research lab. Taylor recalls:

> Fred came back [from the conference] and started talking to the staff members in the lab, primarily Locke Carter and myself, about the possibility of our writing such a program... We tossed the idea around for a month or two, and together we actually worked out some of the technical problems, as well as some of the enhancements that we felt were important for the program to actually be useful. And then, after we had kicked that around for a month or two, I actually sat down and wrote the program. (Taylor, 1989a, interview)

Like Kemp, Taylor was a self-taught programmer, learning BASIC on a Texas Instruments PC he had bought in 1984. He and Locke Carter spent the better part of a day talking through some of the large technical obstacles in writing the program. Indeed, they talked so long that Taylor became hoarse and had to take the next two days off, too sick to teach or to attend class. It was a fortuitous illness. When he returned to the lab two days later, he came carrying the largely completed program code for *Interchange* (the program was then known as *Forum* but would be renamed later).

Unlike the programs from Kaplan's group, Daedalus Group programs are developed first by a principal designer, who then calls upon other group members for input, which he can draw upon as the need arises. For example, Taylor gives Kemp credit for introducing the idea and elaborating on Batson's design, and he cites Carter's technical expertise and working through of major design questions. He admits that he wrote the program without any formal knowledge of social-epistemic theory:

> That [social-epistemic theory] was all new to me then... That's why it's so important to emphasize that this has been a collaborative effort, because others in the lab who were talking about this were familiar with the social epistemic. Fred certainly was, and another one was Wayne Butler, who was around the lab at this time. (Taylor, ibid)

Instead, Taylor, who others in the group describe as a programmer-perfectionist, admits he wrote the program for the "fun" of overcoming the technical challenges: "I enjoy programming, and I enjoy problem solving." He admits that he did not see much use for the program and credits Kemp with the vision of its classroom value. Kemp, on the other hand, gives Taylor credit for being able to handle the tough programming problems posed by *Interchange*'s design: "He's a much more meticulous programmer and much more thoughtful—I'm a very slapdash, hacker-type programmer" (Kemp, 1989, interview).

All of those involved in the Daedalus Group stress the importance of programming knowledge and collaboration. Because each person involved in the development of the *Daedalus Instructional System* could program in PASCAL, with its easily transportable blocks of code, each could contribute to parts of an individual program. Kemp explains:

> PASCAL allows you to take twenty-five or thirty lines of code and dump them right into a program in a way that you can't in BASIC. So, we can use the same editor with *Mindwriter, Interchange,* and *Descant,* and in every other aspect of the larger system. Being able to work together in PASCAL encouraged a whole group of things that we were able to do, which I wasn't able to do working for a whole year and half by myself. When those guys came on board and we started using PASCAL, the production in that lab increased twentyfold. (Kemp, 1991, interview)

Part of that productivity came from a hacker-like sense of play that characterized the group. Taylor says, "We just jumped in and tried things out. By programming, we could see possibilities. We'd write the program, put it in the classroom to try it out, and go from there" (Taylor, 1989b, interview).

The informal collaboration of the Daedalus developers is similar to that in the small-group design work of Kaplan and her colleagues; yet the lack of outside deadlines, the fact that overall design goals do not have to be so clearly articulated at any early stage (as they must be in grant-funded programs such as *Prose*), and the programming expertise of all group members give this development model an air of high creativity. It seems that ideas can "cook" longer in this model, and the program's shape can evolve more gradually. In the case of *Interchange*, an idea comes from an academic conference and is discussed over time by a group of people who are trained both in composition and programming. Each member of the group contributes in different ways: Kemp with the inspiration for the idea and his pushing for its completion, Butler with his theoretical background, Carter with his technical expertise, and Taylor as the principal writer of the actual program. Because the Computer Research Lab included a microcomputer network, the developers could test the program and subsequent changes through actual classroom use. Butler recalls, "We'd come back from class and say, 'We need a larger window here' or 'It needs to be quicker this way,' and then we'd make the changes and try it out again the next day" (Butler, 1991, interview).

The prototype of *Interchange* was completed in 1987, using Computer Research Lab hardware and Taylor's programming expertise. At about the same time, the group, led by Kemp, entered into negotiations with the university over rights of ownership for the software which the group was designing on their own time but on university property. The university claimed exclusive ownership of the software developed by Kemp, Taylor, and the others, and offered no portion of potential sales to the graduate students. Butler says, "I can't remember the details, but it was quite intimidating, and we realized, at that point, that anything we did on university property belonged to them" (Butler, ibid). The disagreement over ownership led to the actual formation of the Daedalus Group and the relocation off campus of all development efforts. The question of software copyright and distribution of royalties is an ongoing one for faculty software developers. Very few institutions have a set policy regarding software ownership, and there are no universal standards among the few that do (Keane & Gaither, 1988, pp. 56–57). In this case, the university argued that it had principal ownership of the software developed in the Computer Research Lab. As a result, the members of the Daedalus Group, which was formed in 1988, renamed all the software they had developed while working in the Computer Research Lab (this is when *Forum* became *Interchange*), rewrote all the program code, and ceased their software work at the Computer Research Lab. Development efforts moved to a room in Paul Taylor's modest suburban home, as did all the operations of the newfound company, though they still used their software in the classes they taught at the university.

Their observations of student users led to further revisions of *Interchange*, with a complete overhaul of the code in 1988. Based on their observations, Taylor and the others simplified the interface and made the message editor a full editor. The latter change was an attempt to make a stronger link between the on-line conversation sessions occurring on *Interchange* and the students' subsequent writing sessions:

> A full editor allows you to load in text that you've already written, or to save parts of the ongoing conversation to a file. The students have always had the ability, after a *Forum* session was over, to get the program and call it up and look at it. But sometimes it's nice to say, "Well, now, this particular chunk, here, I'm going to want later when I'm writing my paper." With the new *Interchange*, they can take that chunk and save it to a file right there, while they're participating in the session, and they'll be able to call it up later. (Taylor, 1989b, interview)

The hypertext component in the program, completed in March 1989, came from students' desire to place their new comments in those parts of the ongoing conversation where they best fitted, as opposed to their only being able to add comments to the conversation chronologically as the comments arrived.

The Daedalus Group members depend on the sale of their programs for funding of their software development efforts and the continued revision of existing programs. As suggested before, this allows them freedom from some of the constraints of grant-funded programs like *Prose*. Because profits from the sale of Daedalus Group software can sustain continued development efforts, the group has been able to continue revising programs in a way that neither Schwartz nor Kaplan has been able to do. The company made its first sale in 1989, but survived on a combination of capitalization (mostly from friends and family) and custom programming jobs for other parties. With the *Daedalus Instructional System* now installed at about thirty-five sites, sales of its programs have allowed the company to move into a four-room office suite on the outskirts of Austin, hire programmers and a half-time administrative assistant, fund a full-time position for Wayne Butler, who is completing his doctorate, and even pay modest dividends to its shareholders. Butler jokes, "I think we surprised even ourselves. I think some of our shareholders were investing for the tax write-off" (Butler, 1991, interview). The group was able to pay Taylor enough of a salary for him to give up his teaching assistantship at the university and devote that time instead to program development.

As a for-profit operation with overhead costs, the Daedalus Group has incentive for producing improved, and hopefully more marketable, versions of its programs. Indeed, its continued success depends in part on Daedalus Group's sensitivity to market needs:

> There's something about a free market. I think we were much more elitist in the beginning, saying, "This is the way we see it needs to be done, and this is the way we'll do it," while we remained in isolation with our twenty or so students. Now, we're becoming much more sensitive to what people want and need and use. . . . There are features, for instance, in the new Macintosh version that are very sensitive to the market's needs—spell checking, style checking, all the stuff we pretty much ignored in the DOS environment. We've got a concordance maker and some of the stuff that is proven and popular; that's what people know about computers and English. Well, we need to meet them [potential customers] halfway, because they're not going to buy the most radical part of Daedalus without something they can start with that they already know. (Butler, 1991, interview)

This is a different dynamic than for *Prose*, for example, which was sold by the designers to McGraw-Hill, effectively removing from their hands the future of the program. Even though the *Daedalus Instruction System* is being bundled with Helen Schwartz's *SEEN* and William Wresch's *The Writer's Helper* in one of IBM's hardware/software packages, the Daedalus Group retains control over the fate of its programs and continues to develop and market them on its own. In contrast, Kaplan expressed great frustration at McGraw-Hill's failure to produce a promised IBM version of *Prose*, which would have opened up the vast IBM-based market for the program.

On the other hand, their software development work has garnered Taylor and the others no recognition or reward from the university or the English department. When asked if he received any recognition from the university for his program-development efforts, Taylor merely laughed. He then said:

> It would be very difficult to say that I had received any formal recognition as a result of that. I have been given travel money to go to conferences to present papers about the software. I presumably would have been given that money regardless of what I was going to the conference for—whether it was to present about software or Milton or anything else. I really cannot say that the graduate program has recognized that particular work in any fashion, no. (Taylor, 1989a, interview)

While it might be argued that conference travel is a form of reward, Taylor and the other Daedalus Group subjects made it clear that they felt the English department, with a few notable exceptions, largely saw their interest in CAC work as a nuisance. This view is in keeping with the experience of Schwartz, Kaplan, and most respondents to the EDUCOM survey.

Professional Software Development

Professional software development by private companies like Dan Burns's Xpercom take the entrepreneurial approach wholly outside of academe. While these design groups operate in similar fashion to the Daedalus Group, a key difference is that the members of the Daedalus Group are academics, first, and program developers, second; members of professional software development teams undertake the task as their sole professional pursuit. It is an evolution that is not out of the question for some members of the Daedalus Group, as Butler admits, and it is a phenomenon common to other disciplines. As such, the professional development of software invites brief examination for the way it illuminates the entrepreneurial approach.

Profits from sales of their software must not only sustain the development effort of the professional developers, but also provide salaries and all of the operating expenses. Those expenses are higher for this design group because it must market products more aggressively, produce more polished packaging, and meet the support needs of a generally more demanding clientele.

Because they have usually severed their ties to academe, the developers, in this approach, enjoy fewer ties to academic research and expertise. While academically based development models derive user feedback from classroom use and observation, the revisions in professionally developed software are more likely to come from customer feedback and market reviews, the latter of which can exert particularly strong pressure on product revisions. Although software for the academic marketplace is reviewed, those reviews are not a prominent part of the journals directed to the computers and writing audience. For example, *Computers and Composition* has not included many software reviews. *Academic Computing*, which is now defunct, did not always include software reviews, and when it did, it buried them in the less-often-read first eight pages of the magazine. In contrast, the trade publications directed to the corporate sector, magazines such as *InfoWorld*, highlight their product reviews, which tend to be lengthy, detailed, and thorough.

Thoughtline's origins, like so much of CAC software, are rooted in the classroom. Dan Burns, the program's sole designer of its original versions, was completing a Ph.D. in English (creative writing) at Oklahoma State University and teaching composition. He also began working for private industry as a speechwriter. While interviewing executive clients for the preparation of their speeches, Burns found himself using a technique that he also used with student writers at the university. He describes this method of student conferencing as "directed discussion":

> This was a heuristic technique for helping students develop essays by asking questions, challenging assumptions, requiring supporting evidence, and then critiquing a final draft.... I found that the technique could be applied not only to topics that I knew of, but also to topics that I knew nothing about. For example, one freshman wanted to do a paper on a rock star I'd never heard of. But I could sit down with her, ask questions, and stimulate her thinking and direct it in such a way that she had something to write.

> These same techniques I used with students can be applied to executive speech writing. (D. Burns, 1989, interview)

While using this method as a speechwriter, Burns came across a 1986 *Business Week* article that discussed uses of artificial intelligence (AI) and its principal programming language, LISP.

The *Business Week* cover story—its photo of the scarecrow from the *Wizard of Oz* poised ready to finally get a brain—promised a revolutionary future, and Burns was hooked. He set out to teach himself LISP:

> For six months, all I did was play with it. I wrote a program that would write poetry and Shakespearean sonnets, and I wrote one that would write erotic fiction—you know, just having fun. And then I began to think about how this could be developed for speechwriters. Now, at first, my goal was to write a program that would write the entire speech—just give it a topic and let it go, a speech machine. (D. Burns, ibid)

Bringing together his teaching experience, his work as a speechwriter, and his play with LISP programming, Burns came up with the initial design for *Thoughtline*.

He soon realized, however, that the idea of a "speech machine" was beyond his reach, so he went to work on the more modest goal of creating a writing aid, one that would help writers develop ideas through a direct-discussion interface. In the development of this first version, Burns operated as a lone program developer. His prototype of that program was completed in 1985, and commercial marketing of the program began in 1986. *Thoughtline* provoked a great deal of interest through reviews in *PC Week, Executive Communications, The Washington Post, Manufacturing Week, MIS Week,* and a host of other publications. Unfortunately, many of the reviews were negative—criticism ranged from displeasure with the program interface, to the print format, to its mishandling of "to be" verbs—so Burns pulled the program off the market.

Given the sophistication of the program and his early failures, Burns knew he needed more technological expertise for a revision of the program. He therefore enlisted the aid of AI specialist Robert Giansiracusa, a graduate of MIT's Artificial Intelligence

Laboratory and an employee of Neurotronics Research Corporation, a Washington, D.C., AI development firm. In a ten-day marathon session of twenty-hour days, Giansiracusa and Burns rewrote the program. In subsequent sessions, the pair changed the program interface, switching to easy-to-use pop-up menus, adding color, and working on the program's editor to allow word wrap. Burns feels, for the most part, that these revisions were superficial but necessary for marketplace acceptability and success:

> We found that reviewers will not focus on what I consider the substantial points of the program, and they won't take it seriously unless it looks like a slick, modern, up-to-date program. So it bothered me that our first task was to make the program look sharp, which we've pretty much done. (D. Burns, ibid)

In the development of the revised program, Burns and Giansiracusa worked as a team, and in July 1988, the program was rereleased as *Thoughtline II.*

In the world of commercial software development, the user feedback which has the most impact on program revision is the published review directed at the target market. Burns discovered this early in the development of *Thoughtline,* when the program was released prematurely. This time, the program received more positive reviews. For example, *MIS Week* called it a "viable writer's tool," and *PC Week* said, "For the hesitant or inexperienced writer, the program offers an attractive approach to combating writer's block." At the same time that Burns and Giansiracusa were improving the program interface, they were making deep structural changes in the program:

> He [Giansiracusa] wanted to write a program that would not only conduct a conversation, but that would learn, and that would do not only syntactic pattern matching, but semantic pattern matching. We're not there yet, but the hooks for that are built into the program. We've made it a lot smarter than its prototype, and so a program like this is never finished. (D. Burns, ibid)

Indeed, the two developers are continuing to rework the program, trying especially to reduce its hefty memory requirements, which, if accomplished, would make it a viable program for that still-significant market of microcomputer owners who do not have powerful desktop systems.

Market interest has affected future revision plans for *Thoughtline*, as academe had shown some interest in the program. The program came out of a business context—Burns's speech-writing experience—so its prompts reflect that orientation. Yet Burns has been getting inquiries about the product from colleges and universities:

> We didn't pay a lot of attention to that market [college] because, in 1986, there weren't a lot of IBM compatible computers with hard drives and 640K RAM in the colleges and universities. And, of course, everybody knows that public education is not as well funded as private business. They can't write a check for $300 quite as quickly. So we thought, "Well, that's fine. If they want to write to us, we'll sell to them." (D. Burns, ibid)

A recent review of Xpercom's customer base reveals that 20 percent of its sales have been to colleges and university faculty. As a result, Burns is considering an academically oriented version of the program for the future.

In contrast to the entrepreneurial model, represented by the Daedalus Group, the professional model of program development, represented by Dan Burns, enjoys the benefit of software sales in a market that can and is willing to pay a higher price for that software. In addition, the professional developer's market allows wider technological boundaries in programming efforts, given the greater technological resources of the corporate sector compared with the average computer writing lab for which the Daedalus Group designs its software. On the other hand, the business market is, perhaps, a less forgiving one. Professional software development is more at the mercy of published reviewers in an aggressively competitive market, while academically based development efforts are characterized by greater collaboration between users, students and teachers, and the developers.

In both cases, the entrepreneurial model for program development is marked by the creativity of people who know composition (or who at least have taught a lot of writing) and who know programming. Selfe asserts the need for both kinds of expertise:

> I would love to have a programmer who knew as much as possible about the content area . . . that's why Paul Taylor is so good. But there have to be content specialists, really, content specialists, not just hackers. English hackers and computer hackers—there has to be a blend of the two. (Selfe, 1989a, interview)

Each member of the entrepreneurial design team provides that blend; thus, their collaboration provides impressive resources for working out problems of pedagogical and technological design. In addition, their profits allow them technological resources not available to faculty designers, who most often have to work with whatever hardware is available to them. Those profits also allow the entrepreneurial design team to operate independently of the constraints of institutional funding, and because it does not hire outside programmers, the group's development costs are significantly lower than those of developers who are not programmers.

The Research-Based Design Team

At the other end of the continuum from lone programmer designers like Mimi Schwartz are the large program design teams whose goals are research oriented. These design and development efforts are centered around complex programs constituted of multiple subprograms. Often, these programs require advanced and expensive mainframe computers and terminals. Such efforts are most common in research- and technology-oriented universities such as Carnegie Mellon, where they receive substantial funding, often from government agencies and private industry. The work of John B. Smith of the University of North Carolina at Chapel Hill, Christine Neuwirth of Carnegie Mellon, and Earl Woodruff of the Center for Applied Cognitive Science all follow this model for program design.

While program ideas in the other models often arise from reflection on classroom practices or from just playing around with the computer, the generation of program ideas in the research model comes from a highly structured, cognitive mapping of the writing process. These cognitive models are based on existing theoretical models and/or original investigative research. For example, the development of Neuwirth and her colleagues' *Notes* program began with a team member's observational research on student note-taking. Neuwirth explains:

> Cheryl [Giesler] did a lot of observational work in trying to build up our understanding of what actually went on in this task. The notion was to identify problem areas in the task for the expert or novice. (Neuwirth, 1989a, interview)

Or, in the case of their *Comments* program, they turned to research on the way students respond to instructor comments on their texts:

> We had an early focus on the users, in which we observed people at work, doing the tasks the way they currently did them, and then we tried to form an understanding of . . . tried to form some representations of that task that we thought would be useful. And so it was very empirically researched—it tended to draw on the theoretical. We drew on cognitive theory, and we drew on the writing process, and we tried to pattern what it was we were seeing. (Neuwirth, ibid)

In each case, design began with a perceived problem in the student writer's cognitive strategies; the programs were created to provide "scaffolding" for that part of the composing process; that is, the programs are meant to help students through those parts of the writing process that researchers have identified as being typically problematic areas.

In the case of Smith's University of North Carolina design team, an elaborate multimodal cognitive model was constructed, based on a synthesis of research and cognitive models provided by Flower and Hayes, Bereiter and Scardamalia, and other researchers in cognitive science (Smith & Lansman, 1987, pp. 5–8). This elaborate cognitive model consists of seven modes, each constituted by sets of processes, products, goals, and constraints (pp. 11–12). The model became the system blueprint for an ambitious multimodal writing program called *WE*, a program which acts as a writing environment, encompassing almost the whole cognitive process of writing as mapped out in the design team's initial research and cognitive theory.

Development of the actual programs in the research-based model is conducted by teams of researchers, who often represent a number of disciplines. The design team behind Woodruff's *CSILE* program, another "environment" program that seeks to encompass the whole of "knowledge building" activities, includes people from psychology, education, computer science, and cognitive science theory (Woodruff, 1989, interview). At Carnegie Mellon, a design team is likely to have two principal investigators, a research associate, two programmers, and a number of graduate students (Neuwirth, 1989a, interview). Team members assume responsibility for various parts of the development process. The same applies to Woodruff's team at the Center for Applied Cognitive Science:

> It's [CSILE] a huge program; there are probably over a hundred different files associated with its execution. Its main heartbeat is the server that manages all user requests for a note or for the storage of a note. You can imagine all that traffic. That was really carved off and dealt with in a very traditional sort of way. We sat down and asked what kind of functionality did we need, what would we need to achieve that, and then we turned it over to an extremely bright CMU graduate, Bob McLean. He took over basic responsibility for the server. And it has a nicely defined role, and you don't have to worry too much. I mean, either it has that functionality or it doesn't, and if it doesn't, you fix it. (Woodruff, 1989, interview)

The complexity of the overall program design and the need for each piece of the program to operate smoothly within the greater program constrain the development style of those team members responsible for pieces of the larger puzzle. One is less likely to have the freedom to "play" in the manner described by Kemp or Taylor. Neuwirth says:

> I've seen that occur at Carnegie Mellon. Not in our shop,

> where that really doesn't happen, because I wouldn't let a programmer do that [laughs]. Typically, we are the principal investigators on grants. That would represent a huge risk for us, to have a programmer go off into a closet and maybe emerge months later. I don't think I'd feel personally comfortable under those circumstances, the way my existence here is constituted. (Neuwirth, 1989a, interview)

An important reason for not allowing a single team member to go too far off on his or her own in the development process is the level of user testing typically required at each step of the development process in this model.

Not only is there less "play" and formalized delegation of responsibility in the research approach to software development, but the nature of the team's interaction also differs in dramatic ways. First, software development is a primary professional responsibility for those involved, and that means interaction is a routine part of the work environment (unlike the 11 p.m. meetings in Nancy Kaplan's dining room). This interaction allows for close collaboration between all team members (no one off working alone, as in the Daedalus Group). At Carnegie Mellon, for example, Neuwirth housed the *Notes* team in a suite of oak-trimmed offices in Baker Hall, a lovely, old, renovated building on the Carnegie Mellon campus. She and David Kaufer, the team leaders, the research assistant, the graduate students, and the programmers were all situated in the same place and could make project discussions part of their daily life:

> We had frequent interactions. We could schedule impromptu meetings as well as our usual weekly meeting. Dave is right across the hall and we're always bouncing ideas off each other. (Neuwirth, ibid)

While the organization of the research and design team appears hierarchal, Neuwirth and Kaufer encourage the team members to offer and challenge ideas and decisions. Neuwirth describes these sessions as times of creative argument, where ideas must be defended vigorously and where people use "every conceivable tactic of persuasion known to humankind." She laughingly recalls a recent meeting:

> Dave [Kaufer] and I sat down with the programmers and

asked, "We want to know whether you believe in this programming concept we want to implement?" And they hid their faces behind clasped hands—you know, the sort of church thing where you go, "I *do* believe!" We regarded that as their personal affirmation of faith. (Neuwirth, ibid)

At the same time that decisions are open to group scrutiny, because the team is working on prototype programs, many decisions, particularly technical ones, are made informally while implementing design goals and may be revisited in later discussions.

On another level, this team approach fosters an interplay of personalities that, while probably being no more complicated than in any other collaborative project, is by virtue of the team's size bound to include a wider mix of personality types. The team leader in one such group, preferring not to be named, complained, "I spend half my day, sometimes, putting out fires and smoothing ruffled feathers that stem from conflicts between group members." He pointed out that, because such groups tend to bring together tenured faculty and graduate students, members of different disciplines, academics and hired programmers, conflicts are almost inevitable. For anyone who becomes a chief developer on a project, attention to personal dynamics can be a challenge. Neuwirth, who confesses to being painfully shy, realized on one project that her position as project manager required her to assume a "booster role." Therefore she read management books that described motivational techniques and, she says, "I'd study these things and try them. It was something that didn't come naturally to me" (Neuwirth, ibid). Those challenges aside, the creative-collaborative energy of the research design team, though quite unlike the playful creativity of the Daedalus Group, for example, is indeed one of the major strengths in this model.

The user testing that takes place here during program development is a much more elaborate process than the informal observation of program use described in the other development models. The more formal and fundamental integration of user feedback is called "participatory design." This approach includes user testing from the program's inception, in the way Neuwirth described their study of student note taking, through each revision of the program, through formal field testing. Woodruff's team members installed their first version of *CSILE* in a public school, where they received feedback from teachers and students. However, in contrast to Neuwirth's team, they validated this more informal feedback with protocol studies of selected students. He explains:

> At that point, we started tracking twelve students—meeting with them every week for an hour—trained them to think aloud, and they became fairly comfortable with this study. And we studied whether the system was helping them or hindering them, and how we could change it in response to that. At that time, then, the program was changing about every six weeks. (Woodruff, 1989, interview)

User feedback and study not only prompted design changes, they also informed the actual shape of those changes:

> We would sit down with the kids and mock it up [a design change] with paper and pencil, trying to see if that was a reasonable way to go about it. We would sit and watch them move pieces of paper around a desktop, trying to simulate the types of connections they were trying to make between pieces of information, and then build, design, a system that would accommodate what they were trying to do, with what we were fairly certain they probably should be doing. And then write that up in code and start following that along with case studies . . . Then from time to time we moved to full-class studies, much larger studies. (Woodruff, ibid)

While the research goals and resources of design teams in the research model allow for extensive rewriting of programs, there comes a point in program development when the bulk of those revisions is complete. At that point, the team members can focus their research efforts on field testing of the program to explore the viability of their original goals.

Perhaps the most ambitious example of such testing is that which is being designed for Smith's *WE* project. Smith's group included an automatic tracking function in the design of *WE* which produces a detailed transcript of a given user session. That transcript records each action performed by the user, as well as its time and other important structural information, such as the location of nodes on the user's program-generated outline (Smith & Lansman, 1987, p. 17). Smith claims that "these data avoid one of the most serious problems posed by think-aloud protocols—i.e., distortion of the user's cognitive processes" (p. 17). The protocol data can be used with a session replay program that allows for the reproduction of the session, unfolding in time, and that can be speeded up or slowed down as the observer wishes. Writers can be asked to observe their own session replayed and to comment on their thinking and intentions for various actions or sequences (p. 18). Currently under development is a "grammar" for parsing the protocols. This grammar would have five levels of functionality. In essence the grammar would

1. Offer a symbolic representation of the protocol transcript produced by the tracker.
2. Take those symbols and map them onto a more abstracted symbol system that would identify operations, such as the create node described in their cognitive map.
3. Map these onto a third level of symbols representing intermediate products, such as isolated concepts, relations, structures, blocks of text, and so on.
4. Infer the cognitive processes used by the writer to construct these products, processes such as recalling ideas from memory, associating them, or encoding them linguistically.
5. Infer the cognitive mode the writer is inhabiting at a particular time, such as exploring, organizing, or structural editing. (Smith & Lansman, 1987, p. 18)

Smith argues that the tracking functions of *WE* address many of the well-documented problems through the use of think-aloud protocols. As mentioned above, he argues that the tracking function avoids the cognitive distortion problem commonly associated with think-aloud protocols. The grammar would also solve the problem with inconsistent protocol generation and analysis, in that all the actions of the writers are recorded and the grammar offers objective analysis of the data (p. 18). With the computer doing so much of the work, Smith believes researchers can work with much larger numbers of protocols than before.

As one might guess, the technical sophistication of programs like *CSILE*, *WE*, and *Notes* requires hardware and software resources usually available only at large universities. They need the memory and speed of large mainframe computers and the screen size of workstations like the SUN 3. This type of hardware, the size of the design teams, the amount of programming involved, and the degree and kind of testing involved in the design effort make the research design and development model very expensive. None of the subjects interviewed would divulge their project budgets, though Smith spoke in terms of $450,000 budgets for development projects (J.B. Smith, 1989, interview). These kinds of funds are likely to come from a combination of government and corporate funding agents, yet the subjects were mostly reluctant to reveal those sources. When asked about the funding sources for *CSILE*, for example, Woodruff said, "I can tell you that there are many. There are seven, but I can't tell you the people who are involved" (Woodruff, 1989, interview). He did say that they included both corporate and educational sources. Funding sources for *WE* are identified in the project's technical reports and include the National Science Foundation, the Army Research Institute, and IBM. The home institutions for these projects may assume some portion of the funding but are more likely to cover overhead costs such as hardware.

While the home institutions provide only a small portion of the development funds, they do tend to provide a reward and incentive structure that encourages participation in such program development efforts. The Center for Applied Cognitive Science offers release time to program developers. Neuwirth says Carnegie Mellon treats software development as they would published research:

> I don't think Carnegie Mellon would provide any sort of reward, promotion, or tenure for a program that essentially implemented yet another text analyzer, only in SNOWBALL rather than PASCAL. It's held to the same standards [as traditional research]. I am one of the few people who is a junior person actually building software tools, and my

> renewal case went through, and that work was acknowledged as contributing to my case. And so, it was supported at the department, college, and university levels. (Neuwirth, 1989a, interview)

These developers enjoy a level of recognition and reward not reported in any other model of program development.

To review then, the research-based design team model of CAC program development is most likely to take place in a research university with access to the technological and funding resources necessary to such a design model. The development effort is conducted by a large, often interdisciplinary, design team that follows a highly structured design protocol that includes extensive user testing throughout the development process as well as after installation of the program in the classroom or computer writing lab. The programs that emerge from this model are likely to be based on cognitive theories of the writing process and may try to account for most, if not all, of that process in their design.

As Doheny-Farina and Odell (1985) point out, the "present" that the ethnographer discovers is not static. It is subject to change, even as it is being described (p. 530). This could be no more true than in the world of CAC software design, for the developments of new technology continue to create new possibilities for software, almost every day. Innovations such as hypertext, object-oriented programming, and AI-based authoring languages open up new doors in the design of new programs and the redesign of existing ones. In addition, the issues of funding, the role of software development within departmental reward structures, the marginality of CAC specialists within the field of composition, and a number of other factors are impacting the models just described. The next chapter explores these forces of change in CAC software development and their implications for the future of program design.

Chapter 4

Forces That Impact CAC Software Design

It becomes evident in the discussion of development models that a wide range of factors influence any given development effort and thus the program which emerges from that effort. As was seen in the case of *Prose*, the way the program was developed, revised, and ultimately used had a lot to do with factors such as funding, technological constraints, and Cornell's treatment of the design effort. The idiosyncratic nature of each program's development was illustrated again and again in the development histories of the programs examined in this study. For example, the fact that James Berlin taught for one year at the University of Texas and greatly influenced Fred Kemp and Wayne Butler, who then provided a strong theoretical influence on Taylor's development of *Interchange*, is a project-specific factor. That said, a number of forces were repeatedly cited by the interview subjects as having either an immediate or a forthcoming impact on software design. In this section, those primary impacting forces will be considered.

While the previous discussion identified the various ways that writing software tools are built, this discussion will examine the forces and issues with which the tool builders must grapple in their respective models. The interview subjects identified three primary influencing forces in CAC development: technology, the reward and recognition systems of institutions and English departments, and funding. By examining these three forces as they exert themselves upon the CAC design and development continuum, both now and in the future, one can begin to determine the kinds of software tools that will be available to writers and teachers of writing and to raise questions about the implications of these tools for the field of composition.

Technology

CAC program designers are faced with a number of choices in the development of their programs. What kinds of tools will they use to build their programs? What capabilities do they want their programs to include? What technological innovations seem available and reasonable to include in their program's final shape? By and large those choices will determine a given program's substantiation, how it will be used, and who is likely to use it. For the interview subjects, the most important technological forces are or will be:

programming languages;

system architecture;

networking and telecommunications;

CD-ROM; and

artificial intelligence (AI).

As Paul Taylor says, "What we are able to do will always be determined by the hardware and, in fact, the programming languages we have available" (Taylor, 1989a, interview). Most CAC developers do not have the funds to begin a development effort by purchasing new hardware and software. This can even be true for well-funded research design programs. Instead, most CAC developers work with whatever is available to them at their institutions. So, for example, if the University of Texas Computer Research Lab had been given unnetworked Macintoshes instead of networked IBMs, Taylor would not have written *Interchange*. What software developers eventually end up with has as much to do with the technology they begin with.

Programming Languages

As was illustrated in the earlier accounts, the need either to learn programming or to hire and collaborate with programmers remains a considerable obstacle for writing teachers who want to develop software. Mimi Schwartz, for example, has considered developing a revision program to complement *Prewrite*, but cites the challenge of finding and working with good programmers as a primary reason for not doing so (M. Schwartz, 1989, interview). However, there was general optimism among the interviewees regarding improvements in programming languages, particularly in the development of authoring software that would allow them to develop sophisticated programs with much less training in programming. The two primary developments allowing for such progress are object-oriented programming (OOP) languages and hypertext software tools.

Object-Oriented Programming

Object-oriented programming (OOP) is not new. It has been used in research for over fifteen years, known best as "data abstraction," but improvements in memory and processing speed are making OOP viable for microcomputer applications. Selfe says, "I think object-oriented programming languages are going to open up programming to nonspecialists" (Selfe, 1989, interview). OOP languages offer a fundamental and efficient alternative to traditional programming languages through their substitution of "objects"—blocks of reusable and easily transportable programming code—for the thousands of lines of code necessary to create functions in languages like FORTRAN or COBAL.

As a design concept or methodology, object-oriented programming attempts to make programs operate more like the human mind, at least as the human mind is understood by researchers such as Marvin Minsky or Philip Johnson-Laird. The objects in object-oriented programming are like Minsky's "frames," cognitive data structures that define stereotypical situations which the human mind then combines in order to understand the world (Minsky, 1981, p. 95). Minsky argues that the mind does not have to work through the extensive lines of definition that form a situation. Instead, it possesses frames, which consist of "default values," blocks of possible responses to external stimuli (Johnson-Laird, 1983, p. 189). The mind, when confronted by problematic stimuli, can combine various frames until the external situation is satisfactorily defined. That new definition can then become part of the mind's storehouse of frames. The more default values with a frame, the more finely tuned the frame can become in response to a situation.

To illustrate, consider a small child learning to name things in its world. Assume it has a frame for "bug," for which the default values include "six legs, slightly round body, walks on the ground, smooth shiny torso, pretty quiet." Another frame is "airplane," for which the default values are "a shape that is long and crossed by another straight part, moves through the air, and is pretty quiet." The child sees a butterfly for the first time and shouts "airplane-bug!" In the naming of the butterfly, the child has created a new data structure, or frame, finding in the butterfly some default values of the frame "bug" and some default values of the frame "airplane," and has combined the two to create a new frame, "airplane-bug," which combines characteristics both of form (shape, legs, shiny torso) and of function (flight).

Rather than creating programs through infinitely lower levels of definition, object-oriented programming employs reusable elements, or blocks, comparable to frames in this analogy. Each block of code, known as an "object," is a set of definitions and functions, the default values of Minsky's frames. They can be recombined in a number of ways to create new "objects," which then become part of the program's library of objects. The two key characteristics of object-oriented programming are the combining of data and function and the use of flexible code modules. Jane Fitz Simon (1989) explains the former:

> Imagine you want to add together two numbers. In traditional computing, you call up the operation "plus," feed in two numbers, and run the operation. With object-oriented programming, instead of calling up the "plus" operation, you call up a number "X," and send it a message, "Add Y to yourself." The data is already imbued with the ability to carry out the command. (A4)

Data structures that combine form and function remove a whole level of program functionality from the developer's concerns. In addition, authoring languages designed with the object orientation offer the user blocks of code. These blocks of code would make up objects that could be used in a variety of combinations to solve problems or to write programs without the programmer having to write code line by line (Simon, 1989, A1). The advantages to the program developer are that the objects always remain the same and are therefore reusable; that they are highly reliable and maintainable; and that they save a great deal of programming time. Parlett is working on a design for this type of authoring system, one which would allow users to create *Confer* programs for any given piece of text they desired.

While object orientation holds great promise, it has its drawbacks. Very practical concerns are the high processing speed and the great amount of memory required to run a program designed with object orientation. When the computer runs such a program, it must process each object in its entirety, even though only one or some of the default values within the object are being called upon.

Reconsider the airplane-bug example. For a computer to replicate that child's creation of a new frame, it would process the default values in the "bug frame" that apply to the new object it is trying to name, the butterfly in question. The default values of six legs, slightly rounded body, and shiny torso would obtain, but it would also process and reject the characteristic of walking on the ground. With OOP, the computer processes needless default values. In contrast, a conventionally designed program would precisely define butterfly, and then the computer would process only that information. Expand this simple example to the world of complex computer programs, and what happens is that programs designed with object orientation have much slower throughput, the speed at which a computer can process program code. OOP enthusiasts argue that processing speed will catch up with the software.

One other concern about object orientation is the question of refinement in program design. Because OOP designed programs reuse objects, recombining them and creating new objects, the programs are employing elements not necessarily designed for their specific programming tasks. To illustrate, imagine we were designing a computer that could play racquetball. When we work on the part of the program that effects a backhand shot, we know that we need to program in the slight upward turn, or twist, of the racquet in the hand. Using an OOP approach, we would look through our library of objects and find one that defines the general action of wrist turning, and within that object, there would be a series of defining defaults. Included in, perhaps, a long list of default values that define the turning of the human wrist, we might find what we need to effect this action, so we employ the object in the backhand subprogram we are working on. We have saved a lot of programming time, because we have not had to write code line by line to effect this movement. However, by writing the code ourselves, we could define a more subtle turning of the wrist—a more finely tuned action. In other words, we can effect a turning of the wrist that is *exactly* where it should be instead of the *close enough* position we might get with a preprogrammed block of code.

If the promise of object orientation is fulfilled, it will have the general effect of producing more high-quality, reliable, and easy-to-maintain software at a lower cost. For CAC development, this could reinvigorate software design by lone faculty program developers and small-group developers in a number of ways. Once these developers got over the hurdle of learning an OOP language like C++, they could develop programs much more quickly than they could with programming languages such as Turbo Pascal or Prologue. In fact, some experts argue that people with little or no programming experience comprehend the concepts behind OOP more quickly than experienced programmers. A development expert for Asymetrix Corporation, John Wood, says, "The initial learning time seems to be quicker for people who have never programmed before" (Johnston, 1989, p. 25). Or, if they continue to work with hired programmers, they could get a lot more programming for their money. In both cases, the quality of programs would be higher in terms of standardization (and thus reusability in other programming efforts), reliability, and debugging (a potentially laborious process in conventionally designed programs).

Authoring programs, the design of which OOP makes much easier, would offer powerful development tools to faculty designers. Authoring programs give nonexpert programmers all the building blocks for designing a program, and allow them to construct these programs without a lot of technical language or expertise. For example, an authoring program for Parlett's *Confer* program (which only works with Walker Percy's "The Loss of the Creature") would give an instructor the basic structure of the program and allow her to gear it to any work she wishes without rewriting the code. In any case, object orientation, and the authoring systems that may derive from it, could stand to empower classroom teachers for the creation of their own sophisticated CAC software, in the same way that BASIC led to a generation of early CAI programs ten years ago.

Helen Schwartz believes that creating software has to become as easy as authoring a textbook before writing teachers can undertake the task in significant numbers. She believes that authoring programs may be the answer:

> It's fairly easy to publish your own textbook. [Publishers] have reps beating the bushes looking for people to do it. They [textbook publishers] have got it down so that producing a textbook is not very difficult or very expensive. Developing software is not cheap, and it is not easy. If it [creating software] can be made as cheap and easy as writing a textbook, it can work—and you can do that with prototyping or authoring systems. (H. Schwartz, 1992, interview)

She points out that these programs may not allow novice developers to do everything they would like to in a program, but as she says, "They're a heck of a lot easier than learning programming." Hypermedia authoring systems are beginning to reinvigorate faculty-based software development, though they have not yet achieved the ease of use and the affordability that Schwartz cites as being necessary for widespread faculty development of CAC software.

Hypermedia

In terms of programming languages and authoring systems, hypertext and hypermedia software development programs demand special attention. (While the former term enjoys currency, the latter is more accurate, since almost no hypertext system exists which does not include nonprint media.) Hypermedia is drawing particular attention from CAC researchers because it so profoundly challenges the conventions of print-based literacy practices. Moreover, and more germane to this discussion, hypermedia systems are significantly easier to use and allow nonprogrammers to create highly complex programs. As such, these systems address one of the major hurdles to faculty-based software development: the cost and complexity of writing the actual program code. As William Wresch says, "The more transparent you can make the technology, and the lower you make the development threshold, then the more people will be willing to spend their nights and weekends developing this stuff. I think that will be the trend" (Wresch, 1992, interview).

Hypermedia, a term developed from Ted Nelson's original coining of "hypertext," describes "the synthesis of diverse forms of information storage and display based on a single computer program" (Beck & Spicer, 1988, p. 220). One of the main features of hypermedia is the nonlinear linking of information, any information that can be digitalized, without altering the original data structure from which that information is taken. The units of information within a hypermedia document or application are called "nodes." A node can be a piece of text, a movie clip, a song or musical passage, a photo image, or a combination of media. Nodes can have multiple electronic links to each other and allow potentially endless paths through the data as a whole. The boundaries between information types are broken down, and the hypermedia environment gives the user a great deal of control in how she wishes to link that information.

The most popular hypermedia program in CAC software design has been Apple Computer's *HyperCard*, designed by Bill Atkinson and released in 1987. The program includes a flexible integrated text/graphical database system, an interpreted close-to-natural-language programming language to operate the hypertext functions, and built-in program features that allow users to make links without having to know the programming that effects those links. Such functionality makes possible the creation of highly complex applications (at least from a programming standpoint), but requires little experience or training to use. Beck and Spicer (1988) report an average learning time of sixteen hours for novice faculty working with *HyperCard* (p. 24). There are many hypermedia authoring systems now available on the market including *Guide* (which actually preceded *HyperCard*), *StorySpace, Folio, VIEWS, Supercard, HyperWord, HyperWriter, HyperTies,* and *ToolBook*. Such systems are already finding wide use in technical writing, and their proliferation is reflected in their sales: $1.6 million in 1987 and $485 million projected for 1993 (Fersko-Weiss, 1991, p. 242).

In CAC software, hypermedia, but mostly hypertext, is beginning to establish itself. The hypertext component in *Interchange*, for example, has addressed one of the most common complaints among users of the program: that "lines" of conversation were difficult to trace because of the first-come first-served structure of the main conference. Now the main conversation not only builds in a linear fashion as comments are added on to the end, but also within itself as new comments are linked within the main conversation.

Anne DiPardo and Mike DiPardo are designing a *HyperCard*-based CAC program that would allow students to write essays with built-in buttons which open up windows that would include the students' asides, further explanations, and other information they wish to link out from the text. In addition, the stacks (the name given to information structures linked out from the surface-level text in a *HyperCard* document) would include help screens and exercises to help guide students through assignments; a file of pictures to help spark brainstorming; a note-taking function that can be referenced later; an extensive file of sample essays, with voice recordings of their authors describing their composing processes; a peer communication function; and an instructor/student messaging function (DiPardo & DiPardo, 1989, p. 30). Donald Ross (1989) imagines hypermedia text programs that will allow students to integrate other media in the creation of their documents:

> We will be able to include visual and sound images and music into our assignments, and expect them to be part of the students' writing. These will not just be "figures" or illustrations, but an integral part of the presentation. In effect, then, the student will be producing a multi-media narrative and commentary. (p. 74)

Aside from the obvious design possibilities suggested in the previous examples, the relatively low cost of hypertext development, and even hypermedia development, allows its integration at all points along the design continuum.

While hypermedia authoring programs have the potential to reinvigorate faculty-based software development in the lone programmer and small-group models, it will still be some time before their full impact is felt. Hypermedia systems are still relatively expensive, though an increasing number of "multimedia" systems are being announced (though merely adding a CD-ROM drive to a PC does not make it a hypermedia system) and the computer industry is decreasing the costs for its products at an unprecedented level. More importantly, there are significant technological hurdles to overcome. Storing video clips, for example, requires huge amounts of hard disc space (three minutes of uncompressed video requires about 90 megabytes of hard disc) and makes networking expensive and difficult. The current state of the hypermedia market is chaotic, with new products and support systems being announced almost weekly but with little standardization among manufacturers. While computer technology has always posed the risk to consumers of nearly immediate obsolescence in any purchase (remember those $4,000 Apples with 64K of memory), hypermedia technology is particularly volatile in this early stage of its development in the microcomputer environment. Advances are being made in compression technology and network transmission speeds, supporting hardware is improving, and industry attempts at setting standards are under way. John Manzelli, technical director for multimedia development at networking giant Ungermann-Bass, says, "In about three years the industry will have reached a stage where software producers can reliably know what they will be working with. When that happens, we'll see an explosion of hypermedia software and applications" (Manzelli, 1991, interview).

While there is little actual hypermedia CAC software on the market, the impact of the technology has been enormous. At conferences and in computer and writing journals, hypermedia is one of the most discussed and lauded developments in CAC software design. Robert J. Beck and Donald Z. Spicer (1988), of

Dartmouth University's "HyperTeam," feel that hypermedia will revolutionize software design:

> Designed for easy handling of multimedia, *HyperCard* has been presented as the harbinger of a new dawn of software engineering by and for the masses. It is a forerunner of so-called "authoring tools" which enable users, other than professional programmers, to design and implement their own information organization and presentation applications. The rapid prototyping and development possibilities available with *HyperCard* suggest that it and similar products to follow will spark a renaissance in educational software design. (p. 23)

And unlike the promise of so many hardware and software advances, which await development of just one more piece of hardware or one more piece of software, hypermedia is on the doorstep now.

System Architecture

Most often, the computers that developers find in their labs are IBM PCs, Apples, or Macintoshes, none of which share a common system architecture. In each case, the system architecture demands different design characteristics in software. Taylor discovered this when he attempted to use a Macintosh to program a simple grammar tutorial he had written for the IBM:

> If I developed an exercise that had to do with pronouns, in my ideal version of the exercise, the main loop of the program would say, "What are we going to do next," and when the main loop says, "We're going to do the pronoun exercise now," that was called up. I knew that my program, my section of code, had complete control over the program and the computer at that point. I started at the beginning of my section and proceeded until something was keyed which said either they quit, or they finished the exercise, or whatever. But I knew that the whole time, I was in control of the program. The Macintosh has what they call an "event-driven philosophy." Rather than saying we're going to set up this sequence of events that are going to happen, like in the IBM, I can't predict everything that's going to happen.

> [In the IBM] I ask for an answer and I don't know exactly how an individual is going to answer, but I know that after that, we're going to move on to the second question and the third question. In the Macintosh, they have tried to give the user as much flexibility as possible, so that you can be in the middle of running your program—the student can be sitting there doing a tutorial on pronouns—and just pause, right in the middle of that, and go over and click on an icon that brings something else up. (Taylor, 1989b, interview)

There are other illustrations of system architecture's importance. Because *Interchange* was developed on the IBM, Taylor was unable to design it so that the user could see multiple conferences at the same time. On the IBM, the user can participate in multiple conferences, but must jump from one to another. This would not have been the case if the program had been designed for the Macintosh:

> Now this [the inability to view multiple conferences] is primarily a constraint of the operating environment itself. This is the way that, well, what I'm thinking of is the difference between an IBM PC and a Macintosh. A Macintosh is set up to handle windows and is designed that way. The IBM really is not. (Taylor, ibid)

However, had Taylor designed *Interchange* for the Macintosh, he would have undercut the program's usefulness as a networked communication program:

> So far, Mac networking has lagged behind that of IBM. I think that they are catching up. But IBM PC networks are currently operating faster and more efficiently than networks on Macintoshes. This kind of program is extremely demanding on a network. You have to have one that works very quickly and efficiently. (Taylor, ibid)

Developers of CAC software are faced with a host of these kinds of trade-offs and decisions.

Even developers who possess considerable expertise and abundant technological resources work within technological constraints. Neuwirth illustrates:

> We haven't reached the point yet where memory is so good that we don't have to worry about it. I can give you some instances... In our own work, in the *Notes* program, we had a serious trade-off between, on the one hand, being able to bring up a note at an unacceptable rate of speed and put it in its own window, which gave the writer more flexibility in terms of placement, and, on the other, giving it its own shape and size, and things like that. We would have liked to had the best of both worlds. We were working with the current memory of the machine, which was 1 megabyte I think. When user testing, we decided that the speed at which it came up was far more important—that the whole thing just wasn't going to fly if we couldn't bring up a note card as quickly as you could in a file index sort of thing. That was definitely a trade-off due to hardware limitations that we were banging our heads up against. (Neuwirth, 1989a, interview)

Because the graphics capabilities (for example, the ability to move and shape the notes windows) use large amounts of memory and processing speed, Neuwirth's design team had to compromise in the program's design and preserve the program's pedagogical integrity.

While the technological constraints that a Schwartz or a Kaplan face are most often based on the computers their students are working with in the lab, the constraints that the research design team faces, and the choices they make to overcome those constraints, may greatly increase the lag period between the development of their programs and their widespread use in computer writing labs. This is largely due to the fact that the way to overcome many technological constraints is through more expensive hardware. To illustrate, consider Smith's *WE* program. Because it is a multimodal hypertext program that allows movement through simultaneously displayed windows, it demands a very large monitor screen (as well as computing speed and memory). As a result, the program has been designed to operate on the Sun Microsystems SUN III, a powerful workstation with a 20-inch screen. The funds for five SUN IIIs would cover the hardware and software expenses of a thirty-workstation IBM lab, a trade-off that most writing programs could not afford. Therefore, programs developed by someone like Kaplan might face technological limitations, but they can be widely used by student writers; programs like Smith's, on the other hand, can overcome their technological limitations, but in doing so, create limitations in their dissemination and use.

Indeed, even though the cost of memory and faster central processors has continued to decrease, programs are becoming increasingly complex, with the use of color, graphics, hypermedia, and networking capabilities making heavy demands on memory and processing speed. An extreme example would be Parlett's *Confer* program, which was actually scaled down for microcomputer use, but at that time which still required 18 megabytes of hard-drive storage, a then very fast 386 processor, and at least 3 megabytes of RAM. Or, if one wishes to include IBM's *Interleaf Publisher,* a premier desktop publishing program, in his or her software library, one would need a 386 machine with 6 megabytes of RAM. To use *ToolBook,* one should have a 486 system, 8 megabytes of RAM, and a very large hard drive to accommodate the program, the *Windows* operating system it requires, and the applications one creates with the program.

Unfortunately, none of the interview subjects were very optimistic that these hardware constraints would be addressed in the near future. There was general agreement that screen size would continue to be a problem for some time to come; that memory would continue to be more affordable, but still a development constraint as programs become more complex; and that while IBM's new OS2 operating system seems to suggest a convergence with the Macintosh system, the lack of standardization will, most likely, not be rectified very soon. While the Apple and IBM partnership agreement of 1991 holds some promise for the future, skepticism runs deep among both CAC specialists and industry experts.

Networking

While there are numerous networking systems, all of them effectively do the same thing, which is to link individual workstations so that they can transfer and share information. Two things have happened to make networked application software more interesting to CAC program designers: (1) the decreased cost of memory and processing speed has made the networking of computer writing labs a more affordable proposition; and (2) the growing influence of social epistemology in composition theory has moved CAC researchers to explore the ways in which networking can facilitate collaboration. Local-area networks (LANs) are not new, but the expense in the past has made them more feasible for the corporate world than for academia. Collier's 1987 study, "Computer Writing Facilities: The State of Art" (Collier, Gerand, Parbs, & Morrison, 1987), asked respondents how they would upgrade their systems, but networking did not show up in the responses (pp. 11–12), even though a later question revealed that 75 percent of the respondents considered networking desirable, while the other 25 percent conceded its future value (p. 35). One of the primary reasons listed for not networking was expense (p. 35). Now that LANs are more affordable even for small schools, there is growing interest in how to use them in the writing class. Writing teachers have discovered the efficiency of disseminating information, the sharing of files for peer-editing, and the use of electronic mail (usually a standard part of the networking software) to facilitate communication between instructors and students.

Those fairly straightforward uses of networks have sparked the interest of CAC program designers. There now exists a small number of first-generation CAC programs designed to take full advantage of networking capabilities. Taylor's *Interchange* program, along with Trent Batson's *ENFI* system and Xerox Palo Alto Research Center's *Colab* tools, allows for real-time conversation on the network. As explained elsewhere, these programs allow for on-line class discussion and can display source texts, including student texts, as that discussion takes place. *CSILE* uses networking to create a classroom database in which all students' notes in all *CSILE* sessions can be saved to create a growing database of community-constructed information. For example, if a class is reading the same article and will write a response to it, individual members of the class can access the database to see what their peers have been thinking and saying about that article. At one field-test site, two classes contributed over 12,000 notes to the database (Woodruff, 1989, interview). Neuwirth's *Comments* program allows a student to use any workstation on campus to send a paper to another student or to an instructor, to get it back with comments, and then to make comments on the comments, and subsequently to begin a dialogue with the original recipient if both parties wish to pursue the dialogue further (Neuwirth, 1989a, interview).

A related technology to networking, and one often used in conjunction with it, is telecommunications. Computers can communicate with one another through the use of a modem, the price of which has come down to under $100 in some cases. Modems allow networks to exist over large geographical spaces. This means that a student can participate in an on-line writing class from home or that an instructor can access student texts from an office or home study. Modems facilitate the formation of electronic classrooms without spatial limitation, as with BreadNet students in a New York suburb, who spent a semester working with their peers on a South Dakota Indian reservation by using telecommunications (Selfe, 1990). This technology is in place and needs to be examined for the ways it might be integrated into CAC program design.

CD-ROM

CD-ROM, which stands for "compact disc-read only memory," is a storage medium capable of holding vast amounts of information. The compact disc, best known as a medium for the digitizing of music, can accommodate a far greater amount of digitized information than the conventional hard drive. One compact disc, for example, can hold the whole of the *Oxford English Dictionary*. Because it is "read only," the information contained on CD-ROM can be accessed but not altered by the casual user. As a result, it can become an increasingly important way to store archival information, and it is seeing increased use in libraries. Indeed, Laub (1986) reports that "CD-ROM, introduced early in 1985, is already the heart of some serious businesses based on electronic publishing of encyclopedias, reference works, professional directories, and other large databases" (p. 161).

Now that archival information can be stored more easily in digitized form, program designers are interested in the ways in which they can give their programs access to this information. Robert Alun Jones's Hypermedia Learning Lab, at the University of Illinois at Urbana-Champaign, is using CD-ROM to support its networked Macintoshes with a growing library of application software and data files (Jones, 1988, p. 24). The Brown University Library catalog is being converted to CD-ROM storage—now 350,000 records with about 20,000 additional records being converted every month—and is available to any workstation on campus through the campus-wide network, BRUNET (Hawkins, 1989, pp. 37–38). The prospect of including program access to archival information is an appealing one for CAC developers. Dan Burns cites it as one of the major development goals for future versions of *Thoughtline:* "With an $85 modem, the user could plug into a database and carry on a conversation, and not just with his own subconscious processes, but with an entire range of authors and their works—millions and millions of articles" (D. Burns, 1989, interview).

While CD-ROMs are not yet common to computer-based writing environments, their price has plummeted as new mass storage media have been announced. Compact Disc-Write Once, Read Many (CD-WORM) and Compact Disc-Read Write (CD-RW) drives are on the market and will allow for much more flexible use of CD technology as a storage medium (and go far in solving the storage demands of hypermedia and other applications that use sound and video). Optical storage devices are also available, introducing unprecedented storage capacity, and while the cost of these newer technologies is still prohibitively high for most writing environments, there is no reason to believe that they, like all earlier computer technologies, will not become more affordable.

Artificial Intelligence

Artificial intelligence (AI) is perhaps the most ambitious goal of computer research. For some it conjures up images of Fredkin's "super-machines," which hardly deign talk with humans (Johnson, 1987, p. 30); however, a more reasonable sense of AI is suggested in its only slightly more modest goal, articulated by Minsky, of "making machines do things that would require intelligence if done by men" (Boden, 1977, p. 4). In educational applications, one might rephrase the goal of artificial intelligence as making machines do things that intelligent teachers do. These instructor attributes would include having expert knowledge of a subject area, the ability to gauge a student's understanding of that subject, and the ability to "implement strategies" for improving the student's knowledge (Burns and Capps, 1988, p. 1). These are the three fundamental components behind intelligent tutoring systems (ITS), or in the area of writing instruction, intelligent computer-aided composition (ICAC). While the prospect of ICAC excites almost all the interview subjects, only those three currently working in that area, Hugh Burns, Dan Burns, and James Parlett, see AI as having an impact on CAC programs in the near future.

Indeed, only three ICAC programs currently exist, *Confer, MINA,* and *Thoughtline,* and only the last is available commercially. There are two formidable hurdles in the development of ICAC programs: (1) the development of natural language processing (i.e., allowing a computer to translate English into machine language); and (2) the problem of defining the knowledge domain. Natural language processing is desirable in any intelligent tutoring system, simply because users can communicate with the program in a language they already know. Indeed, one of the earliest attempts at such an interface, William Woods's *Lunar* program, took place because NASA had assembled a mountain of data about the recently arrived Apollo II moon rocks, but had only a Fortran programmer who could access the information from the computer. NASA wanted geologists to be able to dial up the computer and make inquiries of it in English.

In his effort to create the necessary natural language capability, Woods developed a parsing device called an augmented transition network (ATN), a breakthrough in natural language processing (Johnson, 1987, p. 105). The ATN provided the computer with a mode for understanding and applying the rules of English grammar; in other words, the ATN gave the computer syntactic understanding. That breakthrough was the first important step in overcoming the natural language barrier. However, sentence parsing requires semantic processing in order to make meaning of natural language; the two are inextricably intertwined. Terry Winograd, a leading AI researcher and critic, explains:

> People are able to interpret utterances which are not syntactically well formed, and can even assign meanings to collections of words without use of syntax. This list "skid, crash, hospital" presents a certain image, even though two of the words are both nouns and verbs, and there are no explicit syntactic connections. It is therefore wrong to insist that some sort of complete parsing is a prerequisite to semantic analysis.
>
> On the other hand, people are able to interpret sentences syntactically even when they do not know the meanings of the individual words.... Much of our normal conversation is made up of sentences like "Then the other one did the same thing to it," in which the words taken individually do not provide clues to enable us to determine the meaning without a complete syntactic analysis.
>
> What really seems to be going on is a coordinated process in which a variety of syntactic and semantic information can be relevant, and in which the hearer takes advantage of whatever is more useful in understanding a given part of a sentence. (Qtd. in Johnson, 1987, pp. 117–118)

Winograd's main point is that the natural language puzzle will only be solved when our ability to program the syntactic meaning of words is complemented by our ability to program what AI researchers call "pragmatics," the semantic meanings of language.

Natural language processing has been accomplished more effectively in some fields; intelligent tutoring programs have been developed in fields such as physics, geology, and economics. But in those cases, the knowledge domain can be assigned strictly defined boundaries. For a program in the field of geology, for example, the language base is fairly well defined, and the meanings of that language base are well understood. In composition, the whole world of knowledge is the domain, and thus the challenge for ICAC is the central challenge of natural language processing, the challenge of programming the rhetorical context. This has been most effectively performed in Parlett's *Confer*, because the program deals with a very limited knowledge domain—the text-based analysis of a single short story. In keeping the subject and its analysis strictly defined, Parlett can make his knowledge domain declarative instead of qualitative, the latter knowledge base still being outside the reach of ICAC program design. Hugh Burns has outlined the hurdles for ICAC programs in his 1984 article "The Challenge for Computer-Assisted Rhetoric." He calls for "intelligent systems that have the capability to understand concrete domains and to make inferences" (p. 18). His ideal system will know its uses, its user's writing, and all its variations, and it will know which writing projects are due and for whom—and it will operate with natural language processing.

With somewhat less ambitious goals, *Confer* comes at the natural language problem from another angle. The program plays the role of expert teacher-writer and leads students through a dialogue about a single text, Walker Percy's essay, "The Loss of the Creature." Instead of being built around an ATN or some other parser, it uses complex pattern matching and some lexical equivalents. While this approach is limited for a general natural language processor, it can be made successful when the knowledge domain is restricted enough for the designer to anticipate users' input. The most famous program to use pattern matching was Weizenbaum's *ELIZA*, which simulated the role of a Rogerian therapist, offering canned responses to recognized keywords or strings (Weizenbaum, 1976, pp. 36–45). Pattern matching works in *Confer* because a single essay represents a clearly defined domain; the program can take a student's input and, after breaking it into phrases, match the words in each phrase to a fairly extensive set of words (referred to as "tokens") in the expert module of the program. When a match occurs, *Confer* responds with output determined by the expert module, where the student is in the program, and by the pedagogical rules activated at the time (Parlett, 1987, p. 98). The program performs fairly well in terms of syntactic ability, with an average of one error for every 42.3 lines of system output in the tested prototype (p. 98). Those same tests revealed high semantic performance, with no reported instances of conversational failure or breakdown (p. 114). Given such performance, Parlett argues that "context-sensitive pattern matching does, in fact, constitute a legitimate approach for developing such systems now" (p. 117).

Parlett (1987) argues that the key to making pattern matching work, both in terms of syntactic/semantic performance and in accommodating the world knowledge associated with writing, is to "constrain the content area of the domain of inquiry, only from the system's perspective." (p. 117). The program requests users to make connections between the Percy essay and their world experience, but it does so from the perspective of the program. In other words, it asks users to bring their knowledge to bear on the essay, a domain where it does have expertise. One important effect of that demand is that readers are forced into a close reading or New Critical approach to the story, while other critical approaches are inoperable within the program. Parlett's long-term goal is to integrate *Confer* with an authoring system that would allow instructors to create *Confer* programs for any texts they desired. Such a program would ask questions of the instructor about a given text, building its own expert model for that text. An instructor could create *Confer* programs for an entire semester's reading and then use the program "as a stand-alone assistant to the teacher for these texts, with little further work required on the system for that academic term" (p. 24). In writing courses with narrowly defined constraints, such as the writing of lab reports or, perhaps, technical writing, a *Confer* authoring system might prove very useful.

Unless such an authoring system is developed, my research suggests that artificial intelligence will continue to reside on the periphery of CAC design efforts, largely as a result of expense and expertise. Most AI software is written in LISP or one of its derivative forms. Every statement in LISP is a list or part of a list, usually marked off by parentheses. As a result, even simple LISP programs are difficult to read, even by experienced LISP programmers (Parlett, 1987, p. 69). Because LISP is an interpreted language, it is very slow to process programs. Ideally, it should be run on a LISP machine, a computer designed with a LISP environment and meant to run LISP programs, but these are quite expensive. The Xerox 118 Dandelion, on which *Confer* was written, and its successors cost between $25,000 and $40,000 each, depending on the models purchased and their respective price schemes. Furthermore, because LISP-written programs demand so much memory (in its micro version, *Confer* requires

18 megabytes of hard-drive storage and 3 megabytes of RAM), they are not very portable into the microcomputer environment where most students write.

The interview subjects working in AI are optimistic about its impact in the near future. However, the rest of the interview subjects agreed with Taylor when he said:

> I'm in a camp that says natural language processing is too far away to be of any use to me right now. And I think it may be twenty or thirty years before natural language processing is really developed well enough to handle just any old thing that you will type in . . . I think it's too far away for me to worry about, so I don't put it in my programs. (Taylor, 1989b, interview)

Even those interviewees who work in large design teams, people who are less worried about immediate applicability in the writing classroom and who have good equipment and funding resources, did not see AI as being an impact technology in CAC programming in the near future.

Reward and Recognition

Designing and developing CAC software is a time-consuming and difficult task; on this point, all the interviewees agreed. While there are no consistent, nationwide standards for the treatment of CAC development efforts, research suggests that a lack of reward and recognition is more common at the end of the development continuum inhabited by full-time teachers like Schwartz and Kaplan, than at the end inhabited by researchers and design team leaders like Woodruff and Smith, where reward and recognition are readily available. Given that research design teams account for only a small percentage of CAC software development, the implications of the research are that most CAC software developers suffer from a lack of institutional incentive.

This hypothesis is certainly borne out of the results of the EDUCOM survey on academic software development. Indeed, the findings were rather dismal:

> The results of the interviews indicated that incentives were not generally available to faculty. Release time seemed to be tied to the availability of funds on campuses and, for the most part, was available only through external funding. Since criteria for promotion and tenure were established at the department or school level, there were few campuswide standards that gave credit; others counted it as a publication if it was published; and still others did not accept development activities as promotion criteria at all. Generally, four-year institutions appreciated development only if it resulted in some kind of publication. The potential to improve the level of instruction was not a significant factor. (Keane & Gaither, 1988, p. 55)

Sixty percent of the survey respondents cited a lack of release time as a serious impediment to software development, and 50 percent cited the fact that development efforts did not count toward promotion (p. 56). Keane and Gaither assert that the demoralizing lack of support reported by people like Schwartz, Kaplan, and the survey respondents is the single most important factor "in sustaining decentralized development efforts" (p. 63).

The EDUCOM survey gathered information on institutional-wide programming efforts in the full range of disciplines. Many of the interview subjects indicated that the lack of support reported by EDUCOM is even worse for the CAC program developers because they typically work within English departments. Some argued that they suffer marginality even within the field of composition. Wayne Butler humorously illustrates the point: "I'm an English education person in an English department, teaching composition on computers—I'm the lowest form of life on my university's food chain" (Butler, 1991, interview). Selfe sees CAC work as having potentially a broad impact on composition studies and English studies, but she argues that CAC efforts are largely ignored by both groups:

> I contend that our success in terms of this broader impact is by no means guaranteed, or even feasible, given our particular position within the profession of English studies. A full decade after the birth of computers and composition studies, we are, indeed, part of an exciting intellectual debate; we are discovering fascinating relationships among computers, writers, and teachers of writing. But we are not

> having a generalized effect on our profession; we are not necessarily leading the thinking that goes on; we are not always a focus of professional debate or even curiosity. We are a group of scholars who attend each other's presentations, but who seldom hear our ideas echoed in more general intellectual exchanges. We exist, if you will, on the margin of English studies. (Selfe, 1989b, p. 2)

Selfe sees composition theory informing CAC work, but not a complementary reverse of that influence. She asserts, "It's not a permeable membrane in both ways. It's only permeable in one way" (Selfe, 1989a, interview).

There are a number of forces at work in the marginality of CAC researchers and developers. One of the most important factors in that marginality is that English departments, in very many cases, range from being outright hostile toward CAC work, to simply being unsure of how to evaluate CAC efforts. Consider the case of Wresch, creator of *Writer's Helper*, one of the most commercially successful CAC programs on the market, and a leader in the field. In 1982, he was a tenure-track faculty member at a community college, and his work on the program was progressing well. He recalls:

> I had received an equipment grant from Apple, so I could do some of this work [programming] at home. I also had a contract with NCTE to write that first book, *The Computer in Composition Instruction*. Things were looking up for me as a developer and as someone who was beginning to understand where computers might fit in. My reward from the English department was to be fired because, they said, I was dealing with computers, and I had no business doing that as an English teacher. (Wresch, 1992, interview)

Wresch appealed the decision, and it was reversed, though he became convinced that he would not receive tenure when the time came because he was "messing with computers."

Wresch left the community college for a faculty position at the University of Wisconsin at Stevens Point. More importantly, once there, he joined the computer science department, where he could continue to work on his software program, to work with teachers and computers, and to have those efforts be valued. In contrast to his earlier experience, Wresch went from assistant professor to professor in four years, was given early tenure, and now chairs his department. Switching disciplinary camps was a drastic measure, but Wresch is not optimistic about changes occurring in the reward and recognition structures of English departments. He remembers winning the prestigious NCRIPTAL/EDUCOM award for *Writer's Helper* in 1988, and what he calls "one of the saddest meetings I've ever gone to" after the awards ceremony:

> Those of us who had won an award got together after the awards ceremony, and we were very, very high—we had just picked up a check for five thousand dollars, we had this huge trophy, we had just stood in front of a crowd of 3,000 people who had applauded us, and we were each convinced that they had applauded for us individually. Then we got into a room and talked about development and what it would take, and in discussing our individual experiences, we discovered that what we had in common was that each of us had been working for nearly a decade, each of us had been working largely alone, none of us had been getting support or recognition from our institutions, and we had continued working despite a lot of obstacles. I don't know what to do about institutions. I don't see that situation turning around much. (Wresch, ibid)

For Wresch, it meant finding an environment that was compatible with his interests, and this meant moving to computer science, though he remains quite active within English studies through his activities in professional organizations.

Given the newness of the technology and the lack of any real history of technologically based research in English studies, the work of CAC researchers remains a difficult challenge to the traditional English department in terms of evaluation and reward. Joseph H. Bourque (1983), for example, recalled his department chair's surprise at his request to have one of his programs considered a publication.

In his article, Bourque argues the validity of CAC work toward the advancement of knowledge, and he goes on to set up some standards for considering it as such. Bourque argues that CAC software requires the developer to have a thorough understanding of the field, as well as expertise in pedagogical theory, cognitive research methods, and programming. He also argues that the act of creating a program is essentially the same as writing a manuscript (pp. 69–70). Bourque is not wholly accurate in his argument; the present study, for example, has revealed the ways in which some program development efforts require no programming knowledge on the part of the developer. However, Bourque's guidelines for English department evaluation of CAC development efforts are more helpful. He suggests that evaluation of CAC work and programs be based on:

1. *Substantive soundness.* The program should be based on the latest and best research in the discipline [composition studies].
2. *Pedagogical soundness.* The program should reflect sound and effective classroom practice.
3. *Efficiency.* Just as the length of a scholarly article is not an indication of its quality, a computer program is not to be judged by its bulk.
4. *User friendliness.* The computer program should be easy to use, even for students and faculty who know nothing about computers.
5. *Documentation.* No program should be dependent on the availability of its author for use or further development.
6. *Demonstrated use.* Evidence that a program is being used locally, regionally, or nationally can provide further indication of the worth of the material. (p. 73)

Bourque's guidelines would not be inappropriate for the evaluation of a textbook, and many CAC programs might be considered in that light. Yet, other programs may help redefine our concept of writing, and in a sense, give birth to new pedagogy, new research, and new theory. If these programs are accompanied by significant theory, then the CAC effort has more value than the production of another textbook. The important point, here, is that these kinds of guidelines could help make clear a department's criteria for CAC development work. While the guidelines for any given department will necessarily be geared toward that department and its particular institutional demands, the key is that those demands be articulated and that departments make clear the ways in which CAC efforts will come into play in deliberations over promotion and tenure.

Those discussions are only now beginning to occur because English departments are faced with continuing pressure to integrate computers into their writing curriculum, even when they would rather not. For example, an alumna of the University of Maine recently donated a computer writing lab to the English department, who accepted it only on the insistence of the academic dean. It is more common for English department CAC enthusiasts to be in a fight with other departments over scarce computer resources, but this example points to the kinds of resistance these researchers face within their own departments as well. The pressure to integrate computers into the writing curriculum has led to what McDaniel has called the "white coat syndrome," the hiring of one department member to act as a computer specialist upon whom the pressure of CAC development can be unloaded (Selfe, 1989a, interview). Selfe sees the newly hired CAC specialist as being in a position to force a departmental clarification of policy regarding CAC work:

> I think that when they get hired, people who are in computers are going to have to go to their department chairs. It is going to be the mutual responsibility of the two to clearly articulate in written form the expectations, the professional expectations, of the chair and of the person, so that they don't fall prey to changing expectations. I think we can do that, but we have to take a proactive role. We can't sit back and assume that a department head is going to understand what we know about computers. We have to educate the head, and the head has to educate us about educational constraints, and there has to be a negotiated stance that comes out of that. (Selfe, ibid)

Until that happens, release time, promotion, and tenure will be more readily available for CAC developers in research settings.

When CAC development is tied to research goals, as it is in the cases of *WE, CSILE, Notes,* and other programs developed in the research design team model, the reward value of those efforts is tied to their success in producing publishable research findings. In each of those cases, the programs will not be widely used in writing classes for some time to come. The programs that emerge from the other three models are intended to improve the writing curriculum, but many English departments, as we have seen, place little value on them. If CAC developers are being denied departmental rewards, this may be due to English departments' lack of understanding about the nature of their work, and also because academic culture does not place much value in pedagogical improvement. This was the conclusion of the FIPSE Technology Study Group:

> The conflict faculty face when forced to choose between the rewards of improved learning in a course and the rewards of publishing research results is deeply rooted in the culture of higher education. We recognize that the traditional and most significant system of faculty reward, tenure and promotion based on disciplinary research, is not flexible enough at many institutions to encompass work in developing curriculum. (Balestri, 1988, p. 46)

If CAC researchers focus wholly on the classroom use of their programs and neglect their work's theoretical implications and research value, then their work will continue to be as undervalued as that of any hardworking classroom writing teacher—no matter how effective their programs are in improving or facilitating student writing.

Certainly, while CAC programs proliferate, a review of the literature on CAC reveals a dearth of theoretical work. Perhaps this is due to the newness of the tools themselves; CAC researchers have been so busy trying to understand them that they have not stood back long enough to explore their broader theoretical implications for composition. Selfe believes that "we've been so busy playing that we haven't had time to look back at the field and make those intellectual bridges that are going to increase commerce between the two areas" (Selfe, 1989a, interview). Wresch agrees and sees publication tied to software development as one possible inroad into institutional reward structures: "If article publication is the currency of the realm, that's one way to continue your software work" (Wresch, 1992, interview). CAC development efforts will have to be bolstered with a stronger theoretical orientation, with more published research, if CAC developers are to partake in the departmental reward structure and "legitimize" their efforts within traditional institutional value systems.

Selfe also believes that the marginal position assigned to CAC development work has more to do with deeply rooted ideological orientations than with academe's stress on research over teaching or over humanists' lack of technological understanding. She believes that the rhetoric of technology in the writing classroom reveals a "reformist vision of computer-supported classrooms":

> one in which students are active, engaged, central, and one in which technology is helping teachers address racism, sexism, inequitable access to education, and other disturbing political-social problems now operative in our educational system. (Selfe, 1989b, p. 5)

She sees the rhetoric of CAC as being closely akin to the rhetoric of feminism, each of them being a "highly politicized, rhetorical, persuasive discourse that calls for change and that commits a community of scholars to positive reform" (p. 6).

Drawing on the work of Suzanne Clark, Selfe identifies a fundamental and ideological opposition between CAC research and the values of the discipline:

> Such discourse does not go over well at the academic center of our profession, say, at the latest MLA convention, where logocentric, unsentimental, agonistic values still often hold sway, where our colleagues think that scholarship should be objective, apolitical, and arhetorical. (p. 7)

Clearly, there is CAC work that does not fit the reformist vision Selfe articulates— the network programs that "monitor" writers at work or Smith's WE come to mind. However, the collaboration that comes in a program like *Interchange*, the empowerment of marginalized students which networks and telecommunications can allow, the challenge to notions of authorship in a hypertext environment, and the idea of shared databases like the one in *CSILE* all serve to challenge the traditional value structure of academic discourse. Even the way these programs are developed—*collaboratively*— rejects the traditional value of sole authorship of intellectual property. And when their work is reported on in print, CAC developers speak in terms of fundamental changes to our present understanding of textuality and its management, a discussion generally "couched in terms of hope and change" (Selfe, 1989b, p. 5).

Ted Nelson ascribes the marginality of CAC developers to an even more fundamental disagreement over intellectual orientation than the one identified by Selfe. In his book *Literary Machines* (1987), he uses, as his starting position, C.P. Snow's notion of two diametrically opposed intellectual cultures: the culture of technology and the culture of the humanities. In Nelson's view, English departments lack an understanding of computer technology as discussed by Bourque, and the values of associations like the MLA which Selfe alludes to are only symptomatic of this larger, cultural split. While Nelson's book is quirky and sometimes overstates his position, his characterization of the battle between the "technoids" and the "fluffies" has the ring of truth:

> About the only thing the groups have in common is their shared view of computers [that they are technical] . . . But one interesting aspect of the two cultures is their view of each other in the world. Each sees the other group as "those people in their little corner, unaware of the big wide world." To the Fluffies, this real world is history, art, literature, and the little corner is "technical things." To the Technoids the real world is that of technical questions and ideas, and the little corner is the artsy-craftsy nook of bygone concerns. (Sec. 1, p. 13)

Nelson goes on to argue that the computer, through networking, worldwide databases, and hypertext in particular (Nelson is one of the key developers of hypertext), stands to radically change our understanding of text and that humanists, as managers of text, and technoids, as those who possess the tools to work with the technology, will have to reconcile in order to guide these dramatic changes.

Nelson is calling for intellectuals who can combine the technological and humanistic perspectives, researchers he refers to as "systems humanists":

As far as I am concerned, both the Technoids and Fluffies are in their own little corners. In the broader view, the goals are the long ones of civilization—education, understanding, the preservation of human values—but we must use today's technologies. I call this view "systems humanism." Civilization as we know it is based in part on running water. That system had to be thought out. Similarly, somebody's gotta design waterworks for the mind. But it should be someone who understands the fluidity of thought. (Sec.1, p. 14)

While CAC work is not mentioned specifically by Nelson, CAC developers come very close to fitting the role he describes.

English departments must come to recognize the special role their CAC faculty—acting as "technology critics," to use Selfe's term—play in the reconciliation of technology and the humanities (Selfe, 1992). Such recognition and accompanying support for CAC work would go far in ending the often-decried lack of good CAC software. For even as the EDUCOM survey reported the dismal treatment of CAC development efforts, the survey team concluded that software development continues and that the future of such efforts is promising if the issues of reward and recognition are addressed successfully (Keane & Gaither, 1988, pp. 63–64).

Funding

Developing CAC programs is an expensive proposition. As was illustrated in the earlier discussion, costs are tied to the model of development in use. The lone programming model is obviously much less costly than the big-budget research design effort. The EDUCOM Software Development Survey does provide some sense of general software development costs. For example, the University of Akron estimates the development costs of a one-hour computer instructional module to be about $10,000. To develop one hour of intelligent tutoring software, the California State University at San Francisco estimated about 1,000 hours of development time, at about $50 per hour (Keane & Gaither, 1988, p. 58).

Sources of funding can range from the bank account of an individual developer, as in the case of the prototype for *Prewrite;* to the institutional funding of the sort Kaplan received for the development of *Prose;* to large grant-giving entities like the National Science Foundation (NSF), the Fund for Improvement in Post-Secondary Education (FIPSE), or the Office of Naval Research (ONR), the latter having funded software development efforts at Carnegie Mellon University. Corporate funding, especially from industry giants like IBM and Apple, can also be an important source of project monies. Commercial sale of CAC software does not yet sustain substantial development efforts, though as the market for such software grows and more effective forms of marketing and distribution are discovered, the for-profit sale of software may become a more viable source of development funds. In cases such as Wresch's *Writer's Helper,* which is being used in 3,000 high schools and colleges, sales have provided ample reward for the developer's efforts, yet this kind of success in marketing CAC programs is still quite rare.

Generally speaking, the lone programmer, small design group, and entrepreneurial approaches to program development are either under- or only adequately funded. Research-based design teams enjoy the most generous funding, especially through ties with corporations (which, of course, have a vested interest in their efforts) and with the defense industry. Perhaps because of competition in the former, and the inherent secretiveness of the latter, interview subjects working in the research design model were reticent about discussing their sources of funding. None would divulge their project budgets, although Smith, as mentioned earlier, used a figure of $450,000 to discuss the management of funds in such projects. Woodruff would only identify the number of funding sources for *CSILE,* seven, and say that they were a combination of corporate and educational sources (Woodruff, 1989, interview). Neuwirth identified FIPSE as a funding source for one project, but she would not discuss funding sources further, other than to say they were typically a combination of government and private foundations (Neuwirth, 1989a, interview).

A relative abundance of funding allows research design teams to sustain complex, ambitious projects. However, funding of this magnitude carries with it some considerable burdens. As Smith made clear, spending at this level requires tighter controls and more accountability, adding a greater number of bureaucratic duties to the task of project manager (J.B. Smith, 1989, interview). Projects that carry this type of funding seem to require a more highly controlled development protocol; for example, Neuwirth cites her role as principal investigator on grants as a reason for closely monitoring her programmers (Neuwirth, 1989a, interview). Finally, at least with the corporate sponsors, there can be pressures to bring a product to market before the developers are ready. Woodruff explains:

> As you know, programs of this size are very expensive, and there are very few private agencies that can afford them. So sooner or later, you have to go to the corporate sector. And as much as they would like to assume a philanthropic attitude, they want to see something that will sell their equipment . . . *as soon as possible.* Yesterday wasn't soon enough for them. You've just got to work out that balance. You've got to convince everybody involved that the research is necessary, and that if you push it out before the research is completed, you'll probably have a product that is detrimental to the goal you are trying to achieve. (Woodruff, 1989, interview; emphasis his)

Despite the pressures they may exert, large funding entities like corporations and government agencies will continue to be the primary monetary sources for the expensive efforts of the research design teams. As a result, continued pressure will be brought to bear on research-based programs to serve both market and government needs. Moreover, because most of the major funding entities are interested in advanced research and development, CAC developers with solely pedagogical aims will continue to see very little of that money coming their way.

Software Publication

If faculty overcome the challenges of developing software and actually produce good and useful programs, they still have a crucial decision to make regarding the dissemination of that software. When programs were more modest in scope, the market less broad, and the costs of development lower, faculty-developed programs were often shared for free or for the cost of the diskette on which they were stored. Oftentimes, programs were simply made available on campus networks. As recently as 1988, an EDUCOM survey revealed that "the majority of academic software developed for the curriculum was not published by any of the major book or software publishers" (Keane & Gaither, 1988, p. 51). This state of affairs resulted in poor dissemination of software and little monetary incentive for faculty to continue their development efforts.

However, as the market for CAC software has grown, faculty developers are increasingly turning to textbook or software publishers. Unfortunately, textbook publishers have not served the interests of faculty software developers very well, despite their extensive sales networks. Based on the experience of those interviewed, academic software publishers are doing a much better job of handling faculty-based software, though there are signs that textbook publishers may be growing more sensitive to the demands of effective software marketing. The publishing histories of Kaplan, Martin, and Davis's *Prose*, Helen Schwartz's *SEEN* and *Organize,* and Wresch's *Writer's Helper* generally illustrate the strengths and weaknesses of dealing with textbook and software publishers. Making a program suitable for the widest number of users, keeping up with evolving technology, conducting effective marketing, making royalties and finding capital for ongoing software development, and keeping software theoretically and pedagogically sound are all tied to the choices developers make regarding the dissemination of their software. Programs have lived and died on the basis of those choices, so the evolution of software publishing is of substantial importance in the discussion of faculty-based software development.

Kaplan's experience with McGraw-Hill illustrates the worst possible consequences of disseminating software through a major textbook publisher. In 1988, unhappy with Kinko's Academic Software Exchange's marketing of *Prose*, Kaplan and her colleagues sold the program rights to McGraw-Hill. She is blunt in her assessment of that decision: "Anybody working on software should not publish it with a book publisher!" (Kaplan, 1991b, interview). McGraw-Hill has failed to upgrade *Prose,* in essence making the program almost obsolete in the Macintosh environment. That was never Kaplan's expectation, but the contract she and her colleagues signed with McGraw-Hill allows the publisher to decide when redevelopment of the program should take place. Kaplan explains the problem:

> The environment in which *Prose* has to exist has changed many times since we finished programming the version sold to McGraw-Hill. But in our contract, we were unable to negotiate what I consider to be satisfactory decision points about when redevelopment would begin. And since the company does not understand software, and wanted always to think of it in terms of the cycles by which they produce textbooks, this was not very successful. (Kaplan, ibid)

Helen Schwartz had the same experience with Wadsworth's handling of her program *Organize:* "One of the reasons I signed with them was that I thought they'd keep the software current, which they never did" (H. Schwartz, 1992, interview). Further exacerbating Kaplan and her colleagues' situation was the fact that the original McGraw-Hill version of *Prose* still had bugs in it. The three developers corrected those problems, but McGraw-Hill had already packaged and shrink-wrapped the flawed version of the program and did not want to repackage the manuals with the new bug-free version of *Prose.*

Prose was originally designed for the Apple Macintosh, but McGraw-Hill planned to target the large DOS market by contracting with a programming firm for a DOS rewrite of the program. Kaplan, Martin, and Davis were often consulted during the project, and though they had no direct decision-making power, they strenuously objected to a number of design decisions that the hired programmers were making. Kaplan recalls:

> They adapted a text editor that had no word-wrap capability. Their first thought was, "Well, this will be acceptable. English teachers don't have very high expectations." They said that they had already built some things around this editor and that changing it would be expensive and complicated... They made some programming decisions that were

very bad, and after McGraw-Hill had thrown a certain amount of money into the problem and came up with nothing close to acceptable, they just cut the funding—so, no more money. (Kaplan, ibid)

As a result, *Prose* never made it into the DOS environment, losing a potential market and costing Kaplan and her co-developers potential royalties of some magnitude. Indeed, sales of *Prose* have been light, and McGraw-Hill scarcely markets the program at all.

A different kind of decision on the part of Wadsworth, on the question of copy protection, led to a similar loss of sales for *Organize*, and thus royalties for Schwartz. Piracy, the unauthorized copying and distributing of a software program, continues to be a difficult issue in disseminating software. While copy protection schemes can be incorporated into a program, they often complicate the program's use, affect its reliability, and make it more expensive (H. Schwartz, 1990, p. 26). Wadsworth decided to copy-protect *Organize*, a decision to which Schwartz did not object. Unfortunately, the right-protection scheme Wadsworth employed proved complicated for users. Schwartz says:

The way they right-protected meant that people had to do a fairly complex operation at the beginning, even to get the program to work. So, essentially, it never sold. They started giving it away. (H. Schwartz, 1992, interview)

Because the program was now being given away free, it paid no royalties. Schwartz at least enjoyed an advance on the program. No longer feeling invested enough in the project to pressure for its redesign, as well as feeling frustrated with Wadsworth, she allowed the issue to rest.

William Wresch has had a markedly different experience with *Writer's Helper*, which is marketed through CONDUIT, an academic software publisher. CONDUIT, in existence since 1972, began as a National Science Foundation-funded consortium of universities developing and sharing faculty-developed software on a not-for-profit basis. Now based at the University of Iowa, CONDUIT operates much like any small publishing house, though its not-for-profit status frees it from some of the constraints of profit-making publishers. Wresch rejected large textbook publishers (coincidentally, McGraw-Hill was one those he rejected) to market his *Writer's Helper* with CONDUIT. He says:

> I really made a correct decision in dealing with McGraw-Hill. The more I talked to them, the more I realized they didn't know anything about software, and that if I were to publish through them, I was not only going to publish, but I was going to spend my life training them to understand what software was. So I went with a software publisher because I needed that level of help. (Wresch, 1992, interview)

Even as early as 1983, when Wresch decided to contract with CONDUIT, the consortium had ten years of experience in marketing academic software to colleges and universities.

The experience that CONDUIT had in creating and disseminating software to the college market led to a much more active partnership between Wresch and the organization than in Kaplan's experience with McGraw-Hill. Wresch explains:

> They could give me a great deal of help on what my interface should be. They knew what necessary documentation should be. They had a clear sense of how to turn a product that worked in my classroom into something easy enough to use so that people in other classrooms could use it. (Wresch, ibid)

That consultation extended beyond mere advice to CONDUIT's actually rewriting some of the program code. For example, in order to make the program run faster, they added, by Wresch's estimate, a full 10 percent to the program's original code:

> I found this astounding. They didn't say, "Here are some things you need to rewrite." They just went ahead and rewrote it themselves—and I'm really grateful for that. (Wresch, ibid)

The program was released in 1985 and went on to sell approximately 1,000 copies over the next three years.

User feedback, Wresch's sense of developments in the field of composition, and new technological developments all led to a substantial revision of the program, with CONDUIT once again doing the programming. The result was the release of *Writer's Helper Stage II*, in 1988. Wresch doubled the number of activities from twenty-two to forty-four, updated the interface to include easy-to-use pull-down menus, and made the program modifiable by teachers. A recent extension of this version included six more activities and works within the MicroSoft *Windows* environment. While CONDUIT has always had in-house programmers, their wholesale rewriting of *Writer's Helper* code was a first for them. Molly Hepler, product manager for English and foreign languages at CONDUIT, cites a dual purpose in CONDUIT's willingness to rewrite the program. On the one hand, she says CONDUIT recognized that faculty developers had little time to undertake such work:

> We try to relieve the professor of trying to stay up technically with changes in the field and with new developments. Working in C or C+, making programs network compatible . . . it gets complicated, and it's unfair to expect faculty to keep up with that. (Hepler, 1992, interview)

On the other hand, CONDUIT enjoyed great success with *Writer's Helper* and saw it as the centerpiece of their software catalogue. Rewriting the program in C (Wresch originally used BASIC), which allowed for the new interface and increased functionality, was good for Wresch and for CONDUIT.

CONDUIT's sense of the program's potential was borne out with the release of *Writer's Helper Stage II*. With a renewed marketing effort by CONDUIT, sales of the program doubled, and it is now being used in about 3,000 high schools, colleges, and universities. CONDUIT, lacking the extensive in-the-field sales staff common to textbook publishers, uses a combination of direct mail, advertising in professional media, and convention booths to market *Writer's Helper*. Their sales to date have been quite good for a CAC software program. Because field sales are geared toward direct student sales, possessing an in-the-field sales force is of little help in marketing software. Hepler explains that there continues to be no viable market base for direct sales of software to students:

> Lots of publishers tried to market software. They thought they could package it with a textbook and sell directly to students through college bookstores. It didn't happen. Textbooks are expensive, and adding even $10 to the cost means students aren't going to buy. And, at least for now, institutions are the ones buying the software, not students. Maybe if that right combination of textbook and software package occurs it will generate sales; then we might be at a disadvantage without a sales network—but that hasn't happened yet. (Hepler, ibid)

Moreover, the sales people who represent textbook companies are often ill-prepared to discuss software when a faculty person does show some interest. As most writing teachers know, textbook sales often begin with a knock on the door by the area representative. Usually working out of home offices and trained to deal with print texts, these sales people often have no training in or familiarity with the software program they carry. Indeed, an informal survey of twelve regional sales representatives who carry some form of CAC software revealed that eight had never used their programs, and four had merely seen their programs in "getting acquainted" demonstrations at regional or national company meetings. None could discuss the programs in detail or address anything but the most basic technical questions. Textbook publishers have simply not kept pace with the technology, and that filters down to a large, but finally inept, marketing force who tries to sell a product for which the parent company has shown no commitment.

Commitment to their software offerings was the quality Wresch and Schwartz saw most apparent in CONDUIT's handling of their programs. Schwartz praises CONDUIT's handling of *SEEN* and the collaborative nature of the organization's relationship with her. At the time she entered into an agreement with CONDUIT, she and the editors there had proposed revisions for the program. As they did in Wresch's case, CONDUIT took responsibility for substantial rewriting of the program code. These changes included an authoring system that allowed customized tutorials, on-line examples, an updated interface, and network capability. They also wrote the program manuals. Schwartz, like Wresch, is convinced that CONDUIT greatly improved the program, made it more marketable, and made the program more flexible for the teachers who would use it in their classrooms. She also readily admits that aspects of the program, for example, the networking capability, would never have been included without CONDUIT's willingness to take on the programming work: "I knew that what I could do alone was not as good as what they could do." She adds, "I have nothing but praise for CONDUIT. They are academics, but they also know marketing, and they're very good. I never have to worry about quality control. They understand software" (H. Schwartz, 1992, interview). At least for the time being, software publishers like CONDUIT seem to be highly preferable to textbook publishers for faculty who are seeking a way to disseminate their software. Certainly, Wresch is as adamant as Kaplan in his advice to avoid textbook publishers: "In every case where a bookseller has bought software, the software developer has lived to regret it" (Wresch, 1992, interview).

Will that continue to be the case? There are encouraging signs that textbook publishers, who are showing a revived interest in software, are growing more sensitive to the demands of handling and marketing. The first such sign is the creation of software editor positions within the companies. Kim Richardson, software developer at HarperCollins, is charged with acquiring software products, working with developers, and developing a catalog of programs that include more stand-alone software not tied to handbooks or texts. She says:

> The history of textbook publishers and software has not been good, in large part, because publishers had no history of working with software. They tried to set that work within a book model, and it just didn't work. Textbook acquisition editors were signing up programs they didn't know, that were not developed properly, and that were then not marketed properly. (Richardson, 1992, interview)

In contrast, Richardson's sole focus is software, so she has nurtured her connections with CAC researchers and developers. For example, one of her first projects at HarperCollins was *53rd Street Writer,* a word processor and on-line handbook developed by the Daedalus Group.

Richardson sees textbook publishers coming to value software more than they did in the past:

> The attitude is changing week to week, for the better. In the past six months I've seen a growing awareness of software. Oh, there are people who would rather not acknowledge my existence within the company, but there are editors who are really interested and want to know how software can help their lists. (Richardson, ibid)

While editors' increased interest may still be tied to improving their text sales, it is important to note that Richardson was hired with the specific long-range goal of building a catalog of free-standing software.

One challenge facing Richardson is the longstanding practice of bundling free software with texts as a marketing strategy. While she admits that many editors see this as a way of selling more texts, faculty, accustomed to getting free software with their texts and often expecting it, are another hurdle. They will have to be convinced that software is a viable component of their curriculum and worth their students' dollars. She explains:

> We often bundle free software with texts and many faculty have come to expect it is a catch-22 that isn't good for any of us. It would be better if students purchased software. That would generate sales for us, royalties for developers, and the increased development that would support would provide higher-quality software for instructors and students. (Richardson, ibid)

Richardson's argument echoes The FIPSE Technology Study Group's conclusion that distribution of free software, through many channels, has failed to adequately support ongoing software development (Balestri, 1988, p. 82). With *53rd Street Writer,* Richardson makes the program available as a $9.95 free-standing program or as a $4.96 ancillary to a handbook. It is still too early to tell if the recently released program will enjoy good sales in either format.

Richardson acknowledges that field sales staff are often unprepared to discuss software products with potential customers. They are emblematic of their industry, slowly coming to grips with a technology that does not fit easily within their print-text frame of reference (and in that, they might be said to resemble many in English studies). Moreover, texts are still the mainstay of their sales, and will remain so for some time to come. As Richardson points out:

> Whenever we have a national meeting, we set up a room with computers and all our software products and invite our sales staff to come in and use the programs and get better acquainted with them. But there are so many distractions at these meetings, and the sales people have so many books they need to know, that they just don't get in there enough to work with the software. (Richardson, ibid)

On another level, technology can be a problem. Richardson explains that HarperCollins sales people use Compaq laptops and DOS machines, but that when they are given Macintosh programs, they are unable to use them and learn the product. She partly compensates for these shortcomings by attending computer and writing conferences, engaging in the same "networking" that her colleagues in the software publishing houses, people like CONDUIT's Hepler, use to make sales contacts. In addition, she offers to make sales presentations with the HarperCollins sales staff.

HarperCollins does not have on staff the in-house programmers which CONDUIT can devote to a software project, but Richardson outlines a relationship between faculty developers and the publisher that may avoid some of the pitfalls that beset a program like *Prose*. If Richardson is presented with a program that she finds interesting, she can negotiate with the developer to continue the development and to present the program for a review process similar to the one used for texts. If the publisher accepts the finished product, the developer can negotiate a one-time license fee or a royalty contract, with 15 percent royalties being the rule-of-thumb average for software products for both textbook and software publishing houses. This arrangement offers little improvement over past arrangements, but another possibility is for the publisher to offer an option agreement that pays the developer an advance and gives HarperCollins the first-right-to-buy. That advance can be used to pay for development costs, and it has ranged from as little as $500 to several thousand dollars for programs in which Richardson had great interest. In either case, Richardson has developed a pool of outside programmers and developers who work with faculty developers. She acknowledges the importance of program revision, but points out that the decision to undertake the expense and trouble is driven by the market demand for the product. In any event, she uses a standard three-year term for software contracts, and she argues that a developer unhappy with the pace or timing of program revision could end the relationship with Harper-Collins and enter into a new relationship with another publisher.

After their initial interest in and failure with software, followed by their subsequent loss of interest, textbook publishers are once again showing renewed interest in CAC software. As Richardson says, "Computers are here to stay, and we know that now." And the proliferation of computer writing labs means that the huge composition market needs software products. This time, however, the involvement of software editors like Kim Richardson, the apparent commitment of their superiors to marketing software and developing a catalog of free-standing programs, and the growing interest of textbook editors in software programs suggest that entering into an arrangement with a textbook publisher does not necessarily have to be the disaster it once was for many faculty software developers.

The Future of CAC Development Models

Anyone who works with computer technology makes predictions about the future with hesitance and some anxiety. The technology is moving ahead at dizzying speed, and because that progress is fueled within a highly competitive corporate market, research and development efforts are highly secretive. Yet, my research suggests that this is a critical period for CAC software development, a time when a number of forces have come together to discourage many computer and writing people from creating software programs, even as new technologies have made the actual development easier than before. For the immediate future, there is likely to be a movement up the design continuum away from the efforts of the lone developer model. However, there are, on the horizon, developments which may help mitigate that trend, but probably not for another four to five years, according to the individuals interviewed for this study. Considering the forces at work in the area of CAC software design (e.g., changes in technology, the reward and recognition structures of institutions, funding questions), I would like to suggest the probable direction of the four approaches to development that I identified earlier.

The Lone Developer

As things now stand, the lone developer approach for CAC development is underfunded, goes unrewarded, and is facing increased technological complexity. While many of the best CAC programs now available have been produced by classroom teachers trying their hand at software development, this approach has become increasingly difficult to sustain; almost none of these developers has gone on to create a second program. There are likely to be fewer programs emerging from this model for the time being. Those programs that do emerge will be necessarily limited in scope and goals, even as CAC programming seems to be moving in the direction of programs such as *WE* and *CSILE*, which operate as comprehensive writing environments that encompass the whole of the writing process.

There is disagreement on the place of such "small" programs in a market accustomed to using large, multifunctional software programs such as *Word*, *WordPerfect*, *Writer's Helper*, and presumably, at some point, a writing environment program such as *WE*. Kaplan believes software programs that address only one small part of the writing process will seem unworthy of the time and effort their faculty designers invested in them, especially in light of software that is already available and the expectations of users: "It's very difficult to adopt something that maybe addresses a tenth of what [users] need to do" (Kaplan, 1991b, interview). On the other hand, if writing environment programs are designed to allow the integration of smaller programs, the latter may find a viable place in the design world. This is the position of

Woodruff, who admires these "little programs," as he calls them (Woodruff, 1989, interview). He sees them as "targeted to do one thing and to do it very well," and he believes that "if they do that very well, there'll always be a place for them. I think the total environment will have to allow movement in and out of those programs" (Woodruff, ibid). Since fully integrated writing environment programs like *WE* and *CSILE* largely exist in research contexts, it will be some time before this question is answered. Hypertext authoring programs, however, are quite another matter.

As I have argued elsewhere (LeBlanc, 1992), authoring programs, particularly hypermedia authoring programs, have the power to revive faculty-based software development in both the lone developer and small design group approaches. Apple Computers introduced *HyperCard* for the Macintosh five years ago, and CAC developers are starting to explore more fully its implications for design. For example, Chris Anson (1989), of the University of Minnesota, is currently working on a hypertext version of rhetorical cases, what he is calling "deep cases," complex and descriptively rich scenarios that use banks of accessible information. The DiPardos' (1989) program, described earlier, is creating new kinds of text that aren't possible in traditional print media. John McDaid (1989; 1991) has his freshman writers producing hypermedia essays. Hypertext and hypermedia (as it becomes more affordable) can allow developers to create complex programs right now.

As faculty see and use hypertext/hypermedia applications, and as those authoring programs become even easier to use, there should be an increase in faculty-based software development. Ron Fortune, who is creating hypertext applications that combine manuscript studies and writing, reports just such a phenomenon:

> So often I hear faculty colleagues talking about what they would like to do in their courses, and it makes no difference whether it's a literature course or a writing course; your first reaction is that the ideal tool for doing this is hypertext. After I gave a presentation on what I was doing with hypertext, faculty came up to me and said, "I would like to try this. Can we get together sometime and talk about

it?" I read that as a very positive sign—that the interest is there. (Fortune, 1991, interview)

At my own institution, where we have installed a hypermedia classroom and faculty courseware development facility, an invitation for proposals went out to fill ten available spots for faculty software developers. With no release time or additional support offered, ten faculty from various disciplines, with almost no programming experience, eagerly signed on, with a second group waiting in the wings. To borrow Catherine Smith's (1991) comment, "They seem minds stunned with possibility" (p. 237).

The lack of any real DOS-based hypertext systems has so far slowed the amount of software development being done by faculty, given the huge installed base of DOS-based computers in higher education. As noted earlier, lone faculty developers work with the hardware available to them, and for a vast number of faculty, that is the IBM or one of its compatibles. Apple's competitors have rushed to enter the hypertext market, but as Tim Bajarin, vice president of Creative Strategies Research International, says, "In the Mac arena [the *HyperCard* idea] is understood. In the PC arena, I don't think anybody has any idea of what it is" (Flynn, 1989, p. 21). That was so for some time, but in 1991, IBM introduced its first integrated hypermedia system and this year began shipping its Ultimedia system, the first DOS system to run hypertext applications at a speed comparable to Apple's Macintosh computer. If *ToolBook,* the Asymetrix-produced, hypermedia authoring program packaged with IBM systems, can do for the DOS environment what *HyperCard* is doing for the Macintosh environment, the power to effectively create software will be in the hands of thousands of technology-savvy faculty. Helen Schwartz's *Discourse Detective* and Ron Fortune's manuscript work have both been created using *ToolBook* and hopefully signal the first wave of DOS-based hypertext applications to join the superb work that other CAC specialists like Moulthrop, Joyce, McDaid, and others are doing in the Macintosh environment.

Helen Schwartz envisions a middle ground in which faculty purchase software programs that have built-in authoring systems and that can be greatly and easily modified. In this case, teachers are not building programs from scratch, but can take the existing "frame" of a program, flesh it out, and modify it in ways that are most useful to them. She explains:

> I think the metaphor for the coming decade is going to be "sampling." What we're going to do is learn to build on other people's work more successfully. (H. Schwartz, 1992, interview)

Her point is that the reusability and transferability of blocks of object-oriented program code, and the authoring programs they make possible, will allow the easy modification of existing software. For example, in Schwartz's own program, *SEEN*, teachers can use the built-in authoring utilities to create entirely new tutorials within the program. Given the constraints imposed upon writing teachers, the lack of support or institutional reward, for example, Schwartz does not anticipate the widespread development of software by writing instructors. However, she believes that modifiable software programs will encourage writing teachers to shape software in ways most meaningful to their students, and that giving software users that power will encourage continued diversity in approaches with CAC software.

The Small Design Group

What is good for the lone program designer is generally good for the small design group, as well. Therefore, advances such as OOP, hypertext, and authoring programs, when they become more readily available, will offer the same benefits in this approach as they do for the lone faculty designer. Indeed, the small design group is likely to take advantage of those benefits even sooner. Given their collaborative structure, small-group design teams are able to assemble a broader range of expertise by bringing in diverse specialists. By employing an audiovisual specialist in their design group, for example, they could more easily expand into hypermedia than the writing teacher who has not worked with videodiscs or animators. Because OOP design allows for the independent construction of objects (or *independent* blocks of code), members of the small-group design team can delegate responsibility for portions of the program more easily than they can with traditional programming languages, thus speeding up their development time. Yet, like the lone programmer, they are likely to continue to suffer from underfunding and lack of rewards.

While the small design groups often work with the hardware they find readily available, the fact that their funding is often partially supplied through grants allows them a little more flexibility in equipment choices than the lone developer typically enjoys. For example, Kaplan and her collaborators were able to choose the Macintosh as their architectural base for the development of *Prose*. This flexibility in hardware purchasing will allow small design groups to take advantage of technological developments more rapidly than sole program designers.

There is likely to be more pressure on small design group members to publish research based on their program efforts and use. While that same pressure may be felt by many lone programmers, because small-group developers are more likely to have grant funding, their development efforts are more formalized, often justified in terms of research goals, and more publicly central in their scholarship. In contrast, while some lone programmers may also seek to work that way and have their programs treated as research related, most, like Mimi Schwartz, have treated software as an ancillary piece of course material—that is, a small piece of a much larger pedagogical approach, developed on one's own time away from professional duties, and often produced without complementary research efforts. Kaplan, on the other hand, sees *Prose* as one of her primary scholarly accomplishments and posited it as her "book" in her successful tenure application at the University of Texas at Dallas. Simply put, published research is still the "currency of the realm," as Wresch puts it, and will be necessary if CAC developers wish their work to be the basis for promotion, tenure, or even release time. While this added burden may slow down program development, the need for research results may have the positive effect of forcing more user testing and evaluation than is typical in this model. While the results of this testing should provide valuable research data for program developers who need to publish, it should also result in better program efforts if these developers are afforded the funds to revise their programs.

The growing number of microcomputers in the writing classroom is creating a growing and viable market for the sale of CAC software, a fact reinforced by the knowledge that college microcomputers are overwhelmingly used for the task of writing. A review of the 1990-91 software logbook at the Springfield College microcomputer lab revealed that almost 80 percent of the software signed out was for word processing. As the FIPSE Technology Study Group points out, one source of development funds may lie in more effectively tapping this market through better distribution and marketing of CAC software (Balestri, 1988, p. 82). This may seem commonsensical, but CAC developers' longstanding habit of making their software available for free or for a very nominal fee resulted in a subsequent lack of profit and provided no funds for future development. In a commercial arrangement, "Receipts from the sale of software pay the developers, the graphic artists, and the publisher's expenses in marketing and supporting the product; most importantly, receipts can pay for the development of a new generation of software" (Balestri, ibid). While the gift-giving approach of "public domain" software is endorsed by the FIPSE Group (Balestri, ibid), the expense of program development, the general lack of funds, and the amount of time and effort demanded by program development make such generosity much rarer.

The success of Wresch and Schwartz in working with CONDUIT suggests that the small group may often be comprised of faculty and publishing professionals. Though Wresch and Schwartz both worked as sole programmers through the early development and even initial distribution of their programs, when they joined CONDUIT, the development of their programs became a small-group effort—a highly successful, collaborative one. The effective small-group approach of the future may consist of one or more faculty members together with the editor, programmer, and marketing expert of the publishing company. One benefit of such collaboration would come in having the marketing expertise, sense of user needs, and technological expertise of the publishers included in the early development stages, thus precluding the often substantial program revisions that occur when software passes from the hands of faculty developers into those of the publishers.

The Entrepreneurial Design Group

If these groups can more effectively market their programs, the expanding market for CAC software has the potential to sustain their design efforts, as well as to fund their expanded development goals and their purchase of the technology necessary to meet those goals. Because they self-market their products, professional developers like Dan Burns cannot rely on word-of-mouth referrals and vendor displays at conferences for the sale of their software. Burns has tried direct-mail marketing for academe with disappointing results:

> When we send direct mail to businesses we get about 2.2 percent in sales. To colleges and universities, it's been about 1 percent at best, which is just not enough to sustain the costs of this marketing approach. (Burns, 1989, interview)

As a result, Burns has been forced to tap the academic marketplace through conferences such as the Conference on College Composition and Communication and the Computers and Writing Conference, and has had to subsequently lower his expectations for college sales. For the program, less money means less revision, and Burns has had to delay his plans for an academic-based version of *Thoughtline*.

The entrepreneurial design group, comprised of academics who start their own software company as a separate and secondary pursuit, can more effectively operate with conference and word-of-mouth marketing. They can do so because their software efforts are not their primary source of income, and because their contacts within academe make word-of-mouth referrals a much more effective marketing device than it is for an outsider like Burns. However, they cannot be blasé about sales. For example, the Daedalus Group members, recognizing the amount of time and effort they were devoting to the company, were forced to double the price of their software in 1990 in order to cover their costs. At that, Butler admits that the group's contract programming work kept it afloat until sales of the *Daedalus Instructional System* could finally sustain operations. Profits, if they are abundant, can cover costs and allow such design groups to purchase new hardware and software tools, allowing them to keep up with changes in operating environments and the marketplace in ways which textbook publishers find it harder to do. If profits are scarce, these design groups will find it more difficult to take advantage of technologies that could greatly influence the programs they design—hypermedia, for example.

While their careers as academics insulate entrepreneurial design group members from the vicissitudes of the marketplace, they nonetheless are forced to juggle their software development and the academic pursuits necessary for their professional success. For example, Paul Taylor, recently hired at Texas Tech, admits that his work for the Daedalus Group greatly slowed his academic progress. Taylor also asserts that his work with technology was not viewed positively by some search committees during his job search: "It scared off most of those I spoke with" (Taylor, 1989b, interview). Wayne Butler, who is now on the job market, echoes that sense and has downplayed his technology work in some cases. Once they are hired, the entrepreneurial designers will most likely find it difficult to balance their full-time academic responsibilities with their software development. Fred Kemp agrees:

> I think it's a very tough thing to do. I think to design software with the kind of originality and risk taking that characterized my early days...I believe that with the responsibilities I have and the demand upon me to publish texts, that I don't have the time to take those risks, to play—I mean play in a very serious way, to learn the new programming languages, for example. (Kemp, 1991, interview)

If they wish to succeed as academics, that is, to receive promotion and tenure, and to create CAC software, members of the entrepreneurial design group, like members of the small design group, will have to demand clarification from their chairs on the treatment of CAC work in decisions about tenure and promotion, and they will have to produce publishable research.

It may be necessary for entrepreneurial designers to follow the Daedalus Group strategy of keeping company work and academic work publicly separate. For example, if Daedalus Group members are presenting a paper at a conference, they perform no Daedalus work there, that is, no working in the booth or meeting with interested customers. Butler points out that in some disciplines, a connection between academic life and the outside corporate/governmental world is prized, engineering or business, for example:

> The business school would much rather have the CEO of a corporation as a lecturer in the department, because that person knows about business, has been out there doing it. I think, in the humanities, there's a skepticism about those who would make money from their knowledge, or something like that. (Butler, 1991, interview)

While none of those interviewed expressed a desire to sever their ties to academe, the precedent for such a break exists in other fields, where strong corporate markets exist for academic expertise in program design. It will be interesting, in the next few years, to see if any entrepreneurial design group members become full-fledged, professional software developers like Dan Burns. Butler does not dismiss that as a possibility for some members of the Daedalus Group, though it has not happened yet.

The Research-Based Design Team

Design teams operating in research universities will continue to thrive and may come to represent a larger percentage of CAC development efforts. The research-based design team has played an increasingly important role for a number of reasons. First, being situated in a research university, design teams are in a position to integrate new technologies as those technologies emerge. This is true, in part, because these technologies are often developed in such settings, because the expertise necessary to effect their integration is more likely to be available at research institutions, and because those institutions are more likely to have the funds necessary to purchase new technologies. In addition, because their goal is research rather than the dissemination of software, they are under less pressure to see their product in the marketplace.

As illustrated in the earlier examination of this model, members of the research design teams operate in an environment where their efforts are valued and rewarded. This kind of professional atmosphere will not only continue to nurture design efforts, but it may draw CAC developers who are currently working in other models. Parlett sees this as a distinct possibility:

> I think the whole movement in design efforts is toward cognitive-based research groups like Chris Neuwirth's or John Smith's. They have the money, they have the resources, and they are doing good stuff. Who could blame someone like a Paul Taylor for choosing to work in that environment? (Parlett, 1989, interview)

If Parlett's prediction is correct, then research design teams will not only have the best technological resources available to them, but they may have many of the best CAC developers as well.

Perhaps the most important development in this model is the continued movement toward complex and comprehensive writing environments like *WE* and *CSILE*. The development of a single, cohesive writing environment represents a significant break from previous macro-environments or "macroprograms" like *Writer's Helper,* which offers a diverse menu of subprogram offerings. Macroprograms like *Writer's Helper* or *HBJ Writer* allow their users to pick and choose among subprograms for those that best meet their needs as writers. They can choose "strategies that accord both with individual writing styles and with the demands of both their topics and their intended audience" (Rodrigues & Rodrigues, 1984, p. 85). The pluralism of macroprograms is largely rejected in the new "environment" programs. Parlett explains the rationale:

> This design philosophy [of macroprograms] is characterized by an "objective" or naïve pluralism wherein all instructional methods and strategies for invention or prewriting are treated as potentially and equally legitimate, without regard

for the pedagogical stance enacted by the teacher in the classroom. Such a pluralistic tolerance removes the burden of strategy evaluation from the teacher and places it solely on the students, themselves, who must sample such a mixed bag of approaches in its entirety before adopting one or more strategies for the work at hand. (Parlett, 1987, p. 58)

A strong advocate of Parlett's view, John Smith argues for comprehensive writing environments designed around a highly structured cognitive model of the writing process:

While these programs [CAC software] offer writers new tools, they do so piecemeal and with minimum concern for the large-scale structure of the writing task. Their designs often seem driven more by what the computer can be easily programmed to do rather than by what will help writers most. Badly needed are tools designed from the outset to closely match and to augment the inherent cognitive processes that human beings use to perform the complex, multifaceted task of writing. (Smith & Lansman, 1987, p. 1)

Woodruff's willingness to integrate independently developed "little programs" in *CSILE*, a total writing environment, is not shared by Smith, who urges a stricter adherence to a highly formalized design model (Smith, Weiss, & Ferguson, 1987).

Wresch sees some important design issues in the emergence of writing environments like *WE* and believes that such programs are out of synch with the needs of teachers and the demands of writing classes:

Every teacher I've talked to resists that approach for a very simple reason: you only get students for fifty minutes. What they wanted, and still want, and request from me are activities that can be done in a fairly short period of time. The environment that you create is not the software; it's the classroom. The teacher comes in and says, "Today we're going to do module A or module B," as part of a larger process that they, the teachers, have envisioned as taking place over a week, or two weeks, or three. So the glue that holds everything together is not the software—the software never takes over anything—it's the classroom. The class has to be able to get into a particular activity, to do something the teacher thinks is of value, and to get out again before that bell rings or the period comes to an end. (Wresch, 1992, interview)

Wresch argues that software designers need to keep the teacher central in the design concept, and that software must not only give teachers control over the programs but also empower them to decide what is important for their classrooms. As writing environment programs move from the research setting to the marketplace, teachers, the key consumers in the CAC market, will largely determine the ability of writing environments to find acceptance in the classroom. It will be interesting to see if Wresch's sense of their needs is borne out.

An Overall View

While diversity still exists in approaches to CAC software development, recent years have seen an increase in the number of one-time developers who abandon further projects as well as a general drop-off in programming efforts. One key reason for the decline in CAC software work has been the growing complexity of technology and the corresponding increase in program sophistication. The arrival of authoring tools and hypertext, as well as the decreasing costs of technology, may reinvigorate faculty-based programming on the part of classroom teachers. However, formidable obstacles still exist for those interested faculty and include the marginalized position of CAC specialists, a lack of institutional reward and recognition, and difficulty in acquiring funding. While overcoming technological hurdles is significant, our success in addressing institutional issues will be the key in assigning CAC software development its proper value and in keeping it within the province of English studies.

For now, the increased cost of CAC development and the growing complexity of programs are moving CAC development up the continuum toward the research design model. That model will account for a greater number of CAC programs, though the lag period between their development and their common use in writing classes will remain significant until memory, processing speed, and larger screen sizes become much more affordable. The value placed on CAC program development in university research programs will make it the most welcoming environment for CAC specialists.

The work of CAC developers in the other three models will not be properly rewarded by English departments in the near future, due in part to a lack of appreciation for the intellectual rigors of good CAC work, to some deeply rooted anxieties about technical culture, and to an ideology that devalues work that emerges from the classroom and is meant to improve the curriculum. The research model has developed in an environment where these obstacles are much less pronounced or are entirely absent. Many of the developers working in the lone programmer, small-group, and entrepreneurial group models have been people with no real stake in departmental reward systems. They might be said to have been marginalized in the departmental structure during their program development efforts, being either graduate students (Taylor, Kemp, Carter, Parlett) or working as adjunct faculty (Mimi Schwartz, Kaplan). In the latter case, faculty developers have generally produced only one program, finding the lack of reward and the effort required for program development to preclude new development projects or even revisions of their original programs. In the former case, CAC work has slowed progress in the graduate program and will pose interesting problems for these developers as they enter the profession or decide to pursue another career. The first generation of composition specialists with CAC as their doctoral focus are only now entering the field. In many cases, they are likely to be burdened as their department's "computer specialist," falling victim to the "white coat" syndrome; they will be expected to publish and teach full loads; and they may find very little time for their CAC program work.

Take, for example, the case of Fred Kemp. Kemp was hired by Texas Technological University as an assistant professor. He is director of developmental writing, director of the writing program, the English department coordinator for the Texas Assessment of Skills Proficiency (TASP), and overseer of their expansion of computer-based writing facilities. In addition to that, he is trying to maintain his responsibilities to the Daedalus Group. His colleagues worry. Parlett says:

> It's real hard trying to fulfill academic duties, particularly the way they pile them onto new faculty, especially writing faculty. And then try to do any computer programming? I don't know how Fred does it. It's not the supportive atmosphere I work in at the Human Resources Lab. (Parlett, 1989, interview)

The little time left for program development might drive CAC specialists to research settings that nurture this kind of work. The situation may spark an increase in professional development groups, if the marketing strategies can make that endeavor viable, or it may simply cut down on the number and quality of new CAC programs, forcing some developers to abandon their efforts entirely.

The nonresearch-based design models stand to be reinvigorated by new technologies, hypertext most immediately, but also object-oriented programming and authoring programs. The impact of hypertext is being felt across the whole design continuum and only awaits better DOS-based programs to prompt a whole new generation of software, particularly from the small design and entrepreneurial design groups. However, the complexity of hypertext systems and OOP will dissuade all but the most dedicated lone programmers.

In trying to determine the direction of CAC program development, my research suggests that the work of research-based design teams will play a much more prominent role in the field overall. They have the funds, the technology, and the resources to develop complex programs in an atmosphere that values and rewards their efforts. The success of the entrepreneurial design model will be tied to its success in tapping the growing CAC market. The size of that market is suggested by looking at just one of its parts. Consider the figures:

1. The number of computers used in elementary and secondary schools quadrupled from about 250,000 to 1983 to over one million in 1985.
2. Three-quarters of the schools which had not previously used computers began to do so.

3. During the 1984–85 school year, approximately 15 million students and 500,000 teachers used computers as part of their schools' instructional programs. (Qtd. in Herrmann, 1989, p. 111)

For those academics working in the entrepreneurial model, their CAC work is likely to be constrained by professional duties and pressures. That will also be the case for members of the small design group. In both instances, a change in attitudes by English departments will go a long way to reinvigorating these models. If the success of the research-based model confirms the old adage about the rich getting richer, the lone programmer's fate seems to confirm the second half of the saying. A lack of reward, a lack of funding, and the growing complexity of the technology and design goals are making the lone programming effort a thing of lore, a relic of the days of BASIC and 64k machines.

Chapter 5

CAC Software Design and the New Literacy

While computer and writing specialists may still feel marginalized within the profession, their fundamental belief that technology is radically redefining writing and most other literary practices is taking hold. A growing chorus is proclaiming the digital revolution, as Richard Lanham (1989) terms it. A call to order is being issued within English studies, either directly, as in Andrea Lunsford's 1991 MLA address, or implicitly through the increased attention paid by mainstream journals such as NCTE's *College English* and MLA's *Profession;* the growing number of CAC sessions at the MLA and CCCC annual conventions; or the now steady stream of professional texts from publishers such as NCTE, Boynton/Cook, MLA, Ablex, and others. There was little choice in the matter.

The limitations of print text have become all too nakedly apparent in the light shed by the computer monitor. For example, the transmission speed of electronic text, the ability to move through a hypertextual database and easily reassemble data, and the compact mass storage possible with electronic text are ideally suited to library science, information services, and business. While the return on their investment has been questioned (Moran, 1991, p. 2), American corporations are spending huge sums on electronic communications systems and are adopting technologies such as electronic mail, hypermedia, and computer conferencing at a furious pace. Like it or not, corporate needs and practices exert a powerful influence on curricula in both secondary and higher education, and corporate America's widespread adoption of the computer as a communications tool will have a significant impact on the English classroom. As Lanham (1989) says:

> Some of the billions of dollars American business and government spend to train their employees are being spent in redefining the "textbook"—and, almost in passing, the codex book itself—into an interactive multimedia delivery system. Sooner or later, such electronic "texts" will redefine the writing, reading, and professing of literature as well. (p. 265)

While the profession struggles to understand the changes in its subject area and to rewrite its curriculum, on-line documentation and hypermedia systems have altered technical writing irrevocably and have created the first direct link between the changes in corporate communication and undergraduate education (Shirk, 1991; Zimmerman, 1989; Carlson, 1988; Bernstein, 1988). As Muriel Zimmerman (1989) said to her colleagues in technical writing:

> Many of us will acquire programming skills and write or edit on-line menus and messages. Some of us will become hypertext information architects. Some of us will have facilitating roles in a technology whose outlines we can only guess at.... We may continue to be called writers; modern truckdrivers are teamsters, and firemen ride diesel trains—but I don't think that we will do much of what Thelma Thistleblossom [a Timp Software grammar- and style-checking program] can do, or even much of what we presently do. (p. 245)

Zimmerman's use of the future tense should not mislead anyone. These changes are taking place now, and they serve notice on those of us working in composition that our students must be prepared to function in a world of electronic discourse when they leave our classrooms.

The new literacy has not been thrust willy-nilly upon English studies because of the demands of the workplace; as technology has moved beyond word processing and stand-alone computers, compelling connections have emerged between electronic communication and many of the current theories informing both literary and composition studies. As George Landow and Paul Delaney (1991) assert, the

> deep theoretical implications of hypertext converge with

> some major points of contemporary literary theory and semiological theory, particularly with Derrida's emphasis on decentering, with Barthe's conception of the readerly versus writerly text, with post-modern's rejection of sequential narratives and unitary perspective, and with the issue of "intertextuality." In fact, hypertext creates an almost embarrassingly literal embodiment of such concepts. (p. 6)

This notion of electronic text's ability to operationalize theory, which print text resists, is echoed in a number of recent works. David Bolter (1991) claims, "Not only reader-response and spatial-form but even the most radical theorists (Barthes, de Man, Derrida, and their American followers) speak a language that is strikingly appropriate to electronic writing" (p. 161). Stuart Moulthrop (1991) sees hypertext uniting deconstruction and the production of all text, everything from the freshman essay to the novel.

Similarly, computer and writing specialists have been quick to point out the compatibility of computer-based writing and much of the current thinking in composition theory and pedagogy. In composition studies, Trent Batson (1988) echoes Landow and Delaney's (1991) assertion, claiming that "it was as if some of the current theories about how to write were developed specifically with networks in mind, even though the developers didn't know it" (p. 32). Early CAC research was enthusiastic but often unconnected to theory and larger issues of literacy. In 1989, calling for more theoretical work in computers and writing and the changing nature of literacy, Cynthia Selfe (1989c) wrote:

> Our profession will have to work diligently in the next few years to identify and explore the changing nature of literacy with a computer-supported writing environment, and to consider the implications of these changes for our teaching. (pp. 13–14)

CAC research has begun to take that broader view and has explored more thoroughly the connections between on-line literacy behaviors and theory. For example, in more recent work, Thomas Barker and Fred Kemp (1990) describe the new "postmodern pedagogy for the writing classroom" (p. 1); Janet Eldred (1989) has clearly outlined the way computer-based writing supports social constructivist theory (pp. 209–216); Ron Fortune (1991, interview) is linking notions of intertextuality and revision in his hypertext-based manuscript work; and Selfe (1990) has explored the potentially liberatory effects of computer-based writing for otherwise marginalized students. The proliferation of computer-based writing labs, the installation of campuswide networks, the increasing number of students who now own their own computers, and the enthusiasm of colleagues who teach in electronic environments have all fueled the growing interest in CAC within composition studies.

At present the challenge for CAC specialists is less to convince their colleagues that a transformation in literacy is taking place and more to urge them to assume a central role in defining how technology and literacy will intersect. As John McDaid (1991) puts it:

> It seems we are in the midst of a "phase change" between technologies, when the characteristics of the defining medium become momentarily apparent. . . . Here is an opportunity and, for composition theorists, a responsibility. (pp. 217–218)

Henrietta Shirk (1991) echoes McDaid's call to order, and she voices one of the key points of this book when she says, "If those concerned about communication do not participate in the development of new theories for the new technologies available in the field, others will accomplish this task for them" (pp. 198–199). The argument needs to be extended, for even Shirk relegates composition to a reactive position when we are in this unique, yet perhaps short-lived, even ignored, period that allows us to shape the technology through software development and thus become proactive in the shaping of the new literacy. We confront, then, a question of vision, or more precisely, a question of whose vision we will be working with in our classrooms.

Relying on Corporate Creativity

Writing teachers could wait for the computer industry's hardware and software manufacturers to create products in response to their needs, but such a stance ignores the longstanding relationship between technological development and consumer need, a relationship in which technology drives need (some would even say dictates), not the reverse. Nancy Kaplan (1991a) treats this subject with great insight, reminding us that complex technologies arise within existing and self-perpetuating ideologies that have the capital and power to shape those technologies (pp. 21–24). She echoes Richard Ohmann's (1985) assertion that "computers are an evolving technology, like any other, shaped within particular social relations and responsive to the needs of those with the power to direct that evolution" (p. 680). The key to shaping consumer need is to make the original technology seem "natural" to its users, so that all subsequent needs and consumer feedback begin with the base technology and its underlying assumption of "what can be," to borrow from Goran Therborn. If consumers of technology begin to define their needs in terms of the base technology, with its sets of capabilities and limitations, their sense of what could be is constrained from the outset.

Consider just one of the technologies that has inspired so much interest and enthusiasm in CAC: networking. Networking has made possible Barker and Kemp's post-structuralist writing classroom. It seems to make possible new pedagogies based on social constructivist theories of writing, in which collaboration, empowerment, student-centeredness, and social-based learning can be realized. Yet network technology was first designed for military and then business use, and its design favors security, hierarchical relationships among users, and surveillance. At best, writing teachers must work to overcome those obstacles; gaining full freedom from them might even mean building a new network technology from scratch, as occurred with *CSILE*. In another example, Ron Fortune, working with *ToolBook* to create hypermedia applications in the DOS environment, complains that the software belies IBM's business orientation and has required him "to work around" those limitations (Fortune, 1991, interview). Because we do not create hardware (though Ontario's development of the ICON computer was a valiant attempt), computer and writing teachers will always be subject to *at least* that amount of ideologically influenced technology in their on-line environments.

Indeed, if the microcomputer were designed in response to writers' needs, it would most likely look and operate quite differently than it does now. Screen size, which affects reading effectiveness and thus revision, as Haas (1989) has shown, would have allowed long ago more than an average of fifty-one lines of text on a screen. Kaplan comments:

> Where did the architecture of the IBM system—which still, by the way, dominates the world as far as I can see—where did that come from? Well, it certainly didn't come out of anybody's notion of how people actually work with text, yet that actually turns out to be the single most important application of microcomputers. My favorite example of this is the notion that documents scroll down. Where did that come from and why is it so deeply embedded in the architecture of all word processing? How did it get to be that way? Well, it almost doesn't matter how it got to be that way; that it is that way really shapes our relationship to emerging text. (Kaplan, 1989, Interview)

Selfe shares that view, points out the computer's military-industrial lineage, and suggests that the computer embodies elements of that background:

> What are the command lines that come up on the computer? They've been somewhat disguised in the later years: "Abort, kill, zap, and execute." Every command line comes right out of the military background of the computer. My suspicion is that it's reflected in many other subtle ways. (Selfe, 1989a, interview)

As writing teachers who are exploring electronic literacy and struggling to answer the question "What can be ?" we might find that the range of answers available to us is already constrained by what has been offered and what we accept as our starting point.

In the worst case, those underlying design values result in networked systems like Robotel's *MicroSelect* video network system. Marketed at educational conferences, the system allows teachers to monitor their students' screens, unbeknown to the students, and to interrupt and take over a student terminal. Note the pedagogical values implicit in the following excerpts from their marketing materials:

> No More Inattentive Students.
>
> The teacher can end the class' work at any point by preempting their screens . . .
>
> Better teacher control over student work.

Computers tended to interfere with age-old, proven pedagogical techniques. ("*MicroSelect:* The Essential Tool") This particular product seems the computer embodiment of Bentham's Panopticon, against which Selfe (1989b) warns. As she explains, the Panopticon was Bentham's design for a circular prison with a guard station in the middle, constructed in such a fashion as to allow guards to observe prisoners unobserved by the latter, creating a king of paranoid self-discipline in the prison population (p. 10). As Selfe says:

> We have not acknowledged or explored the fact, for example, that these electronic spaces [networks] can be used as "disciplinary" technologies, through which teachers control students and their discourse in the most traditional sense. (p. 10)

Technologies like *MicroSelect*'s network system, merely an extension of the underlying technology's design and ideological basis, undermine the promise of electronic literacy. A reality of computers and writing, and one not likely to change, is that the tools the computer industry affords us are ideologically laden, as Kaplan, Ohmann, Olson, and others would argue, and that ideology may often conflict with teacher ideals and goals.

Forging Alliances

While collaboration between academics and corporate interests is common and often valued by some disciplines, for example, business, engineering, and some medical fields, those relationships are fairly new to the humanities (though manning the conference booth of one's textbook publisher carries some of the same reverberations). Within the humanities such relationships have been forged most directly and visibly in computers and writing studies. For those working in research settings or in some software development programs, these alliances are as necessary as they are in any field that relies on what is often expensive technology and equipment. For example, the Computer Research Lab at the University of Texas was founded on an IBM equipment grant, and without it, the Daedalus Group would not have come into existence or created its software. Similarly, Apple Computers has given substantial support to the *CSILE* project, and the computer William Wresch used at home to first create *Writer's Helper* (then called *Essay Writer*) was provided with an Apple grant. Such funding has made some of the best CAC software possible, but it is, of course, in the hardware manufacturers' best interest to support software that moves their product line.

Collaboration with corporate interests seems to inspire a complicated mix of reactions within the CAC community. Because that collaboration can mean financial support, knowledge of and early access to new technologies, and endorsement of one's work, there is a measure of pride and prestige for the faculty person; CAC faculty have been featured in "resource" materials produced by both Apple and IBM, and both companies have featured faculty-developed software, the latter producing potential sales of the software and royalties for the developer. Other perks might include travel to corporate-sponsored conferences, consulting opportunities, and employment possibilities. However, many within the humanities look askance at such partnerships and see them as exploitive relationships in which academics sacrifice their scholarly objectivity. For now, given the lack of institutional support and funding for CAC software development, collaboration between developers and corporate interests seem a necessary, if complicated, arrangement.

Wresch, who has forged those corporate ties as visibly as anyone, asserts that such relationships are good for the companies, with their need for the guidance of academics, and are good for the academics, with their need for support and technological know-how. He agrees that a hardware manufacturer like IBM is looking for software that "it can sell and runs on its machines... that enhances its product," but that computer companies also have a sincere and well-intentioned interest in education:

> They want to market to us, and they need to understand [the academic marketplace], but some of it is altruistic, as well. They are interested in who their next generation of employees will be, what kind of a school experience their own children will have. They're interested in education for more than simply making money, and that's true for all of the hardware companies I've spent some time with. They honestly do listen. (Wresch, 1992, interview)

Wresch also points out that companies like IBM and Apple have hired many academics who go on to play key roles in shaping academic technology for the manufacturers:

> If you say you work with IBM, or you say you work with Apple, generally who you're working with is somebody who used to teach at a university and is now employed over there, so you're essentially talking with one of your colleagues.... Because they come from our milieu, they're not hard to talk to. They know exactly what's going on over there [academe], because they were, in many cases, over here for a decade or two before they went over to the company. These individuals come out of an academic tradition, they are hired at some point by the hardware companies, and they understand our needs. (Wresch, ibid)

Wresch focuses on the individuals who represent the corporations, people with children, academic backgrounds, and perhaps similar values, and anyone meeting someone like IBM's Doug Short, a former medievalist, or Apple's Rich B. (last name kept confidential at his request), who works on educational technology for children, is struck by their thoughtfulness, intelligence, and idealistic vision for computer-based learning. That said, Apple and IBM are still large capitalistic entities that exist to generate profits, and the intersection of that ontological fact and our educational purpose bears further consideration and ongoing diligence.

Military Funding

While corporate affiliations are not entirely new to English studies—many faculty have contracts with textbook publishers and do consulting work—military funding is another matter. Given the military's longstanding investment in computer technology, it comes as no surprise that the military invests in software development. For example, the Army Research Institute has sponsored John Smith's work with *WE*, the Office of Naval Research funded the construction of Carnegie Mellon's software development center, and the Air Force and NASA have begun a joint hypertext project. Within CAC software development, Department of Defense (DOD) funding, which can be quite substantial, has occurred only within the research design approach, yet some of those interviewed think such funding should be avoided.

Reservations about DOD funding have been raised on many campuses and within many disciplines, but the issue had not arisen within composition or English studies until the advent of CAC software development efforts. Interview subjects were more guarded in their comments about DOD funding than they were about any other subject—in part, I believe, because the CAC community is still quite small and therefore has less room to accommodate the kind of ethical and moral recriminations often engendered in this debate. One interviewee, under promise of anonymity, said:

> It's not that the software someone produces with military funding is itself good or bad, it is just that on one level, such developers are buying into some larger enterprise in which the military sees their software playing some functional role, and on another level, there is ethical complicity in that larger enterprise as well. There are no neutral technologies.

Chris Neuwirth acknowledges the ethical reservations held by some of her colleagues at Carnegie Mellon toward DOD funding, but she applies a more practical principle to the question as she pursues project funding:

> Richard Young put it this way to me, when I was first

starting. He said, "Chris, don't ever go out and get money where you wouldn't do what you're doing anyway." That's the bottom line we use to judge whether we are going to go after it [funding]. If it's something we would do anyway, and the [funding] constraints aren't shoving us in a particular direction, then it's okay. I can say that this has been the case for our funding. (Neuwirth, 1989a, interview)

Unlike the affiliations with corporations, which take place across the development continuum, partnerships that rely on defense funding will likely remain within the research setting, where they are less controversial and more actively sought; this is not, however, to dismiss the issue, for if broad-based faculty development of CAC software continues to decline, the research setting stands to play a more influential role in articulating our vision of computer-based writing.

The Ascendancy of Cognitive Theory in CAC Design

As writing becomes increasingly an electronic practice, the dominance of any one approach to computer-based writing in the CAC software market has important implications for all of composition studies. Kaplan (1991a) illustrates the power of software to shape our thinking about information and knowledge making in her discussion of electronic databases:

> The database's underlying structure, usually invisible to the user, shapes both the forms inquiry can take, and for what purposes. Anyone first encountering an electronic cataloging system bumps up hard against such reality as he or she struggles to transform strategies appropriate for a system of card files into new mental habits for a system dependent on Boolean techniques. And the nature of those habits depends on the software's data structure and on the user interface constructed by the software's designers. (p. 15)

While Kaplan does not mention it as an example, consider the influence exerted by *Lotus 1-2-3* on the business world. It has now become almost mandatory in undergraduate business programs to teach *Lotus 1-2-3*, the most popular spreadsheet and database program in existence. Because training in *Lotus 1-2-3* or one of its imitations is almost universal, the program has largely come to define the way a whole generation of business people understand spreadsheet and database management. If composition studies does not find ways to support faculty-based software development, to encourage and reward faculty for learning and using new hypertextual and OOP-based authoring systems, and to nurture diversity in software design, then the only approach to CAC software development may be that of the research-based design team.

Certainly, the trends examined in the previous chapter suggest that programs in the research-based design team model will account for a larger percentage of CAC programs in the future, either directly or indirectly, and that those programs will be more technically powerful than many of those originating in the other design models. The movement in the research-based design model toward writing environment programs, which operationalize a cognitive theory of writing, also tends to leave little room for accommodation of smaller programs that are likely to be technically and theoretically incompatible. The prospect of CAC software development being dominated by cognitive-based research teams is not a healthy or encouraging one, not because those groups aren't doing some wonderful and valuable work, but because there is great value in carrying over the theoretical diversity that characterizes composition studies into CAC software development. Otherwise, a single, dominant approach to software will allow technology to shape writing instruction as it takes place in computer environments. Instead, writing teachers should be able to choose from the widest variety of software tools possible and to shape their own virtual writing spaces.

Diversity in Composition Studies

Since Richard Young (1978) and Maxine Hairston (1982; 1985) argued for the existence of a "paradigm shift" in writing theory, it has become commonplace to refer to the movement from "current-traditional" (Young, 1978, p. 30) to "process" approaches to composition. Such a shift, they argue, is accompanied by and even sparked by the "development of new theories which are able to provide more adequate solutions" to the crisis that undermines established paradigms (Young, 1978, p. 35). That these theories are often competing, contradictory, and include a wide range of research methodologies and aims has been generally accepted as part of a paradigmatic transformation in which the new paradigm struggles to define itself through testing and debate, establishing its boundaries and frontiers through theory and research. In that defining process, the various theories somehow coalesce over time, with some becoming more central for their explanatory power while others fall by the wayside. Until that process is complete, the argument goes, a diversity of approaches should be nurtured. Even adherents to a particular theoretical approach, cognitivists such as Bereiter and Scardamalia (1983), for example, argue for this pluralism in the field:

> On the one hand, we are impatient, as surely many others are, with the miscellaneous character of so much writing research, with its orientation toward topics or methods rather than toward goals, and with its generallack of cumulative force. On the other hand, we think that in this era of competing methodologies there is a special need to promote tolerance and a free spirit of inquiry. Writing research is new, and there is not much of it. It is not easy, and there are, as yet, no magic keys to an understanding of it. Writing research needs to be varied without being unfocused, guided by theory without being dogmatic, progressive without being mindlessly trendy. (p. 3)

Implicit in this passage is the value of diversity in theory as well as in research. It should be noted that some see this diversity is undermining the attempt of composition to establish itself as a discipline. Stephen North (1987) writes, "It might not be too much to claim, in fact, that for all the rhetoric about unity in pursuit of one or another goal, composition as a knowledge-making society is gradually pulling itself apart" (p. 364). A far more common view, at least for now, is Stephen Witte's (1983) belief that various approaches to composition studies, using a range of methodologies, come together as a "cumulative" body of knowledge in the field.

Composition's accommodation of theoretical diversity has been paralleled in CAC software development, as a review of existing programs reveals. For example, *Prewrite* and *FREE* reflect expressivist pedagogies; *Interchange* and *Thoughtline* support social-epistemic theory; and *WE, Notes,* and *Comments* are cognitive-based programs. Indeed, as Janet Eldred (1989) has pointed out, the marketing of the microcomputer and CAC software has thus far paralleled movements in composition studies. First there were "current-traditional" programs that checked spelling and mechanics, programs like *Grammatik,* to be used on personal computers. At that time, the programs developed for these private machines were expressivist, but then both the hardware and the software gave way to more social concerns, manifested in networking, telecommunications, and bulletin boards, as seen in programs such as *SEEN* and *Interchange* (p. 202).

While no single theoretical approach to composition dominates the software market, the subjects interviewed for this study suggested that the increasingly important role played by the research design teams in CAC software production will indeed favor cognitive theories of writing over other competing theories. Parlett, in fact, believes such a phenomenon is occurring at present:

> Things are moving in the direction of design programs like CMU's [Carnegie Mellon University]. In terms of leading development efforts, the cognitive people are really taking charge. (Parlett, 1989, interview)

There are a number of reasons for the preeminence of cognitive theory within the research design model. The connection between the two has developed as a result of the longstanding relationship between computers and cognitive science, and the impact of cognitive science on composition theory.

Cognition, Computers, and Composition Studies

Psychologists have attempted to write programs that model human cognitive processes for almost as long as computers have existed. Such models, it was argued, would offer theoretical explanations for observed human behaviors. One example of such an attempt was Edward Feigenbaum's 1959 project in which a computer was programmed to model the processes by which humans can memorize a list of nonsense syllables (Weizenbaum, 1976, pp. 162–163). While a computer could be easily programmed to perform such a task, "simulation" programs like Feigenbaum's are not performance oriented per se. Instead, they try to reveal possible cognitive processes by successfully modeling them in a computer program, by doing the task as a human would, not as a computer could—the *a priori* assumption being that on a most fundamental structural level, both the human mind and the computer program process information in the form of effective procedures. Thus, if a computer can be made to perform some task *in the same way a human might*, then the computer program can be said to be a cognitive model of how humans perform that task.

One of the most influential projects using computers to simulate human cognitive processes was Simon and Newell's *General Problem Solver,* an information-processing system that sought to model human problem-solving behavior. Positing writing behavior as a form of problem-solving, Flower and Hayes (1981) adopted much of Simon and Newell's information-processing model to develop a cognitive model of writing behavior. Represented in graphic form, their cognitive model resembles a computer flow chart for an information processor; but of course, in this case, the information processor is the human brain (Flower & Hayes, 1981, p. 370). The connection is one straight out of Simon and Newell's work: "All humans are information processing systems" (Newell, Shaw, & Simon, 1957, p. 64). Part of the appeal of Flower and Hayes's work, and some might say, part of the problem with it, is the clearly schematized representation of this otherwise difficult to understand activity we call writing.

From an earlier discussion we know that computer programming requires a highly defined procedural map of the activity that is being programmed. That simple technological fact gives the cognitive basis for CAC program design a great deal of appeal. Within the discourse of computer programming, Flower and Hayes's model could be understood and appropriated as an underlying structural foundation for building computer tools. No other theory of composition offers such a highly defined mapping of the writing process, and metaphors like Elbow's (1973) "growing" (p. 22) and "cooking" (p. 53), for example, are antithetical to the highly defined procedural outlines of computer programming. As Kemp says, "When you program an activity, even the simplest activity, you must be procedurally accurate" (Kemp, 1989, interview). Not only does the cognitive approach to writing lend itself to CAC programming efforts, but it was making itself most strongly felt at the same time that the first flood of microcomputers was arriving on college campuses. Given their currency at the time, and their complementary and longstanding relationship, cognitive theories of writing and computer-aided composition came together in the research setting.

Since then, and for reasons cited in my discussion of design models, the best-funded and best-rewarded CAC projects have been the cognitive-based research programs, those programs which have closely followed the theories of cognitive psychology. Woodruff is working under the auspices of Bereiter and Scardamalia, Neuwirth acknowledges the strong influence of Flower and Hayes, and Smith has based WE on a synthesis of cognitive models that includes Flower and Hayes's, Bereiter and Scardamalia's, and others. Indeed, Smith's opening statement in Smith and Lansman's "A Cognitive Basis for a Computer Writing Environment" (1987) neatly resolves the question of competing theories:

> During the past ten years, our understanding of writing has changed significantly. It was in 1980 that Dick Hayes and Linda Flower first outlined what has since become a standard model for both composition theorists as well as cognitive psychologists who study writing. (p. 1)

Obviously Smith overstates the case, and he admitted as much in his interview, but he does hold a firm conviction that the cognitive approach is the right one *and* that CAC design confirms it and will drive that conviction for the rest of the field.

This was made most clear in his keynote address at the 1989 Computers and Writing Conference, where Smith echoed North's critique of composition's claim to being a viable discipline. Like North, he argued that a lack of methodological soundness and an unfocused and centrifugal body of research have characterized composition; that to survive as a discipline, composition required a more clearly delineated research agenda, methodology, and practice; and that all three existed in the development of cognitively based computer tools such as *WE*. Smith (Smith & Lansman, 1987) criticizes those kinds of "little programs," as Woodruff calls them, which are typical of the other three design models and that are designed to address only part of the writing process, programs such as *Prewrite* and *Organize:*

> While these programs offer writers new tools, they do so piecemeal and with minimum concern for the large-scale structure of the writing task. Their designs often seem driven more by what the computer can be easily programmed to do, rather than by what will help writers most. (p. 1)

He argues that CAC developers must design programs around the inherent cognitive processes that constitute the activity of writing:

> Badly needed are tools designed from the outset to closely match and to augment the inherent cognitive processes human beings use to perform the complex, multifaceted task of writing. The nature of the interaction between tool and tool user for computer writing invites, perhaps demands, a reconciliation between cognitive research and system design. (p. 1)

Arguable in this passage is Smith's assumption that we can discuss an "inherent" and thus universal set of cognitive processes and his assumption that cognitive methodologies will do more than model them—indeed, that cognitive research can positively identify them. However, it is more useful here to note that in Smith's view, the paradigm shift is complete with our adherence to a cognitive approach and methodology, a theoretical stance that by nature precludes the diversity of approaches advocated in the earlier quoted passage from Bereiter and Scardamalia.

Smith's attempts to capture and address the large-scale structure of the writing process have driven the concept of a "writing environment." *WE*, which stands for "writing environment," is based on a closed model—a multimodal cognitive model that accounts for every aspect that Smith and his associates identify as taking place in the writing process. The program's hypertext capabilities allow for recursive movement through each of the program's modes. Therefore to allow for the inclusion of a program like *Prewrite* would be to disrupt the unity of the model and the very structure of the program. Besides, Smith's conviction that his model of writing is closer to "right" than the models suggested in noncognitive approaches to composition makes the inclusion of these other approaches or subprograms not only unnecessary but theoretically unsound. Unlike the "macroprograms" that reflect the current diversity of approaches in composition theory, writing environment programs like *WE* rigidly adhere to a single approach. If these programs go on to become preeminent in the field, their rigidity effectively devalues the approaches they reject.

The Influence of Cognitive-Based CAC Programs

Indeed, the software that emerges from the research design team model stands to exert great influence on the shape of other CAC programs, creating a ripple effect down the design continuum. This is so because, by nature, their design efforts are most advanced in terms of technological sophistication and capability. They therefore effectively set an agenda for the use of these technologies as they later become available to developers with more modest resources. Neuwirth has seen that dynamic with *Notes, Comments,* and ANDREW, the Carnegie Mellon-wide area network system upon which the program ran:

> ANDREW is now being used at several places and it has had a tremendous impact in the computer science world. For instance, it's the Open Software Foundation file system they chose, and things like that. (Neuwirth, 1991, interview)

She imagines her group's research as creating a sound basis for the commercial software development of others. She says:

> Our model is sort of like ... well, you know, the first outliners were built in computer science, and they eventually made it to the marketplace years later, where, now, most word processors have some sort of outlining capability. That's the sort of influence we'd like to have, where someone reads about our work in a journal, and they're building stuff, and they're a commercial outfit, and they would say, "Yeah, let's try this!" (Neuwirth, ibid)

This "trickle down" relationship with industry, which draws upon research from product design, gives the research team's findings a kind of product validity beyond its own theoretical soundness. Certainly, as writing lab directors search for good CAC programs, they will be drawn to these programs as the most technologically sophisticated, as the most tested, and as the ones endorsed by the corporate computer sector.

This is an unsettling eventuality for some of the interviewees. It should be noted that most of the interview subjects expressing such anxieties were reluctant either to discuss or to elaborate on them. As with the aforementioned subject of defense funding, the nature of the CAC community made those interviewed hesitant to level criticism at any predominance by the research design teams. That said, Kemp worries about the impact of programs developed by research design teams.

> We need computer-based research facilities in English departments—not in every department, perhaps—but I see these things [CAC development projects] being relegated to Carnegie Mellon and Rensselaer and Michigan Tech. I don't think it's right for English departments to assume Carnegie Mellon is going to be able to work for them because, for all the respect I have for Carnegie Mellon and the New York Institute of Technology and Michigan Tech, they are still operating, I think, under certain kinds of assumptions, and we have slightly different assumptions. (Kemp, 1991, interview)

Another researcher (who wished to remain anonymous) echoes Kemp's anxieties about cognitive-based CAC programs dominating the software market:

> A research institute like Carnegie Mellon has a limited vision

that I don't want to see limiting software. If their research is any indication of what their software is going to be, I don't want to see it entering . . . I don't want to see it being the only vision.

Helen Schwartz, who was a Dana Fellow at Carnegie Mellon, expresses unbounded admiration for the work of Neuwirth and her colleagues (as did virtually all of those interviewed). However, she expresses fear that the software emerging from research design teams will too narrowly define the writing process for students and teachers:

If I'm afraid of anything, it's that the software will only come out of Carnegie Mellon or Stanford, because I think there are other models [of the writing process] and that, at the very least, people have to be able to modify software for their students and their classrooms. (H. Schwartz, 1992, interview)

Schwartz encourages software development within a variety of approaches to writing because of the way that software programs can inform and shape each other:

Carnegie Mellon students are a particular type of student, and they're wonderful, but as some have argued, if we in academe don't create our own software, then we will be stuck modifying software designed for the business world. So the same argument applies: in our own world, we need more than one orientation, and we shouldn't rely on modifying the software created at a Carnegie Mellon. Chris Neuwirth is the best. She knows programming and she knows rhetoric, but she has a particular orientation—I mean, she can't do all things. (H. Schwartz, ibid)

Research design teams should not be blamed for their success in software design. The anxiety expressed by many was not that cognitive approaches were somehow wrong, but that conditions existed which discouraged software design by faculty with other theoretical approaches to composition.

Diversity in Cognitive Approaches

If Smith's solution to the diverse nature of composition research is to hold higher the banner of cognition, there are other cognitive research design teams that seem more open to integrating other theoretical and pedagogical approaches. Woodruff's sounds like a social epistemic when he describes the benefits of *CSILE*'s shared database of user notes:

> So the idea of authorship can slip away, or has to slip away. You can get credit for an idea if you want it, but the real power of the system is that everyone is trying to build, and you're part of a community of knowledge builders. (Woodruff, 1989, interview)

Schwartz asserts that the Carnegie Mellon researchers are more open to diverse theory than they are given credit for. Indeed, at the 1989 Computers and Writing Conference, researchers from Carnegie Mellon offered presentations such as "Design and Implementation of a Computer-Supported Collaborative Writing Curriculum," "Creating the Dialogue: Using the Network to Initiate Collaborative Learning and Writing," and "Extending the Dialogue: Using the Network to Evaluate and Support Student Writing." These program developers, all working within a cognitive research model, were at least starting to explore social-epistemic concerns and to act upon them in their program design.

Returning to Smith's *WE* program for a moment, it is interesting to note that he, too, acknowledges in the technical reports a "situational analysis" mode as one of the principle modes in his cognitive model. However, it is the one primary mode *not included* in the design of *WE*, leaving it for the writing instructor to address separately in class (Smith & Lansman, 1987, p. 16). He does point out that he has collaborated with Catherine Smith on three heuristic procedures for evaluating rhetorical concerns, and that they may, in the future, "be combined as a mode and included in the program design to address extrinsic concerns" (p. 16). The last phrase belies a social theory seen through the lens of cognitive research.

WE's limitations aside, it is interesting to speculate on what seems to be an opening up of cognitive-based programs to the area of social epistemology. Selfe believes it is a matter of researchers responding to current thinking in the field:

> I think those people are responding to an interest. What drives the profession is that the profession comes up with interesting topics that it buys into for a year or two, or three or four, or maybe a decade, and this constructs the thinking of the members of the profession. And because we are intelligent human beings, we transport that to our work. (Selfe, 1989a, interview)

Selfe's explanation points to another phenomenon that may help explain this widening perspective of the cognitive research developers. If a shift in the field can effect a rethinking of computer tools, then certainly a shift in technology has the same potential. Simply, the technology necessary to program a social-epistemic approach—the networking capability and the processing speed and memory required to drive it—has only recently become affordable for computer-based writing labs. In addition, technological developments like hypertext are underscoring post-structuralist notions of intertextuality, giving that theory a kind of technological validity and a place in development efforts. Linking computers through networks, or telecommunications, presents a substantial expansion of the market for producers of the appropriate hardware and software. These are often the same corporate funding agents for the research design projects. As Woodruff pointed out, these corporate sponsors want to see software that will sell their product (Woodruff, 1989, interview). Therefore, we have a theoretical basis, a market basis, and the funding pressures for the integration of social-epistemic components in the research model.

In a phenomenon quite the opposite of Smith's insistence on a solely cognitive model for writing, there are indications among some of the interview subjects that the boundaries between theoretical approaches are breaking down in CAC programs. When asked if he felt this were so, Woodruff responded:

> I think so. I think I would use different categories [than cognitive and social-epistemic]. For example, I might want to know if you are trying to be reflective with ideas at one time, or whether you are trying to expand them. [Here Woodruff is referring back to the activity of accessing the community database.] I'm not even stating what those tasks are. I'm stating that I think we don't have a very good

understanding of that at all. And neither one of those fits comfortably. I think investigating networked environments will probably tell us more about that. (Woodruff, 1989, interview)

While none of the subjects could describe concretely how the reconciliation of generally exclusive theories might be made operational in a program, those who commented felt that developments in hypertext and a better understanding of the dynamics behind networked collaboration would help shed some light on the possibility of such a reconciliation taking place. In all cases, it was clear that the subjects were not positing a "macroprogram" of the sort Rodrigues and Rodrigues (1984) describe (p. 85), but rather a theoretical synthesis of traditionally competing theories of writing. That synthesis of theory may be more a hope than a reality in current CAC programs, but the desire to at least reconcile theories of context and cognition are powerfully voiced by Linda Flower (1989) for the field of composition in general:

> We need, I believe, a far more integrated theoretical vision which can explain how context cues cognition, which in its turn mediates and interprets the particular world that context provides. (p. 282)

Because such a synthesis of theory for CAC development would have to find application in a program capable of handling a broad base of concerns, the writing environment programs being developed by research design teams would seem to best lend themselves to embodying a new hybrid theory of composition. However, it remains to be seen whether a synthesis would, in fact, represent an integration of theories or a co-opting of one by another.

Giving Shape to the Future: Some Reflections

English faculty conduct research, design curricula, and write textbooks, and those activities largely define our understanding of written communication. In an age of electronic literacy, the software we and our students use will be a significant part of our pedagogy and may or may not embody a theory or ideology to our liking; thus we have an important stake in its development and design. English teachers in the virtual age must have a variety of quality CAC software programs from which to choose, a variety that reflects the full range of theory and pedagogy within composition studies. In the more distant future, as writing classes take place not within the physical confines of a classroom but in electronic or "virtual spaces," software will more wholly define the characteristics of that writing space (Bolter, 1991; Moran, 1992). Peter Elbow's *What Is English?* (1990)—his reflections on the 1987 English Coalition Conference—offers pluralism of theory and approach as one of the few certain answers to the title's question (p. 117). As the accounts in the present study reveal, that pluralism is at risk within the field of CAC software development. Commenting on the lack of good educational software, Stephen Jobs, co-founder of Apple Computers and NeXt Computers, calls for faculty leadership: "Faculty are the experts. They are the people driving the educational experience, and it's going to have to come from them" (Sprecher, 1988, p. 128). In composition studies, that leadership, once energetic and widespread, is almost nonexistent due to the combination of factors examined in chapter 4.

It would be unfair to underestimate the power and ability of teachers to make use of software, any software, in the best possible ways. Yet, imagine how much richer their classrooms might be if they had the means and support to create their own software, to answer the problems they see in their classes in the ways they know best. Ron Fortune agrees:

> It's extremely important that software applications respond to defined problems and needs, so that someone can say, "Well, this software will help me do something or get at something in ways I can't otherwise do effectively." That's why the people who teach the courses have to develop software. Because if they're the ones articulating the problems, it's difficult for someone out there to develop the right software for them. That's why I started using hypertext. (Fortune, 1991, interview)

In the traditional writing class, teachers fine-tune their pedagogy and materials to suit the particular problems or challenges of a class or an individual student. That may mean using some parts of a text and skipping other parts, copying handouts, renting film, and a host of other ways teachers exert control over the media of their pedagogy. Software, however, does not lend itself so well to such tampering, particularly if the designer leaves out the mechanisms for teacher control that Schwartz and Wresch, for example, include in their programs.

Many with whom I spoke were pessimistic about the chances for any revival of widespread faculty development of software and for good reason. Despite technological developments that will allow even nonprogrammers to create complex software, departments and institutions continue to undervalue those efforts, funding is still difficult to acquire, and obstacles remain to effective dissemination of finished products. In developing an understanding of electronic literacy—supporting computer and writing work, in general, and software development, specifically, and training writing teachers for the new literacy as well as supplying them with the appropriate technology—composition studies is not keeping pace with the computer's growing adoption as the communication technology of choice for the workplace and the classroom. This is the context in which faculty find themselves. The accounts gathered for this book capture, in large part, the state of faculty-based software development at the end of the 1980s and beginning of the 1990s, but as Stephen Doheny-Farina and Lee Odell (1985) remind us, "No matter how carefully and thoroughly the ethnographer studies the life of a particular group, the details of that life will continue to change" (p. 530). There is much that can be done to revive and nurture faculty-developed software, and some of that groundwork is being established at present.

While no single, concerted effort is being made to address the aforementioned problems facing faculty software developers (and there may be few who recognize the issue), a number of developments are encouraging. On one level, there is a growing acceptance of computers and writing studies and its importance within the discipline of composition studies. This is evidenced in Lunsford's presentation and the other instances mentioned at the start of this chapter. In addition, the language of computers and writing studies is coming into the lexicon of composition studies. For example, the forthcoming NCTE-sponsored *Encyclopedia of English Studies and Language Arts* has a technology section and a full range of entries, and the new *CCCC Bibliography of Composition and Rhetoric* includes a section on computers and writing. It will become increasingly difficult for composition theorists to ignore computer-based writing in their work, particularly as the sites for their research become electronic writing environments.

On another level, the field of computers and writing is maturing. While much of the early research was more enthusiastic than sound, much of the recent work has been original, rigorous, and has contributed to a widening understanding of computer-based writing. As a result, the subject has begun to receive more attention in mainstream journals such as *College English* and *College Composition and Communication*. While there have been brief periods of heightened attention paid to computers and writing in the past, the current revival of attention is more likely to be sustained as many of the leaders within CAC studies come to play more prominent roles in composition studies in general. One recent example is Cindy Selfe and Gail Hawisher, editors of *Computers and Composition* and the series which is copublisher of this book, being named editors of the new *CCCC Bibliography*. Recent attempts to address software issues have included a special issue of *Computers and Composition*, a revised version of the NCTE Software Evaluation Form, and new bibliographies of software and software-related texts.

Perhaps the biggest change in the thinking about software development will be heralded by the development of hypermedia and its accompanying authoring systems; they present a powerful combination of intriguing pedagogical and theoretical possibilities combined with relative ease in use. As the authoring systems become even easier to use and as the platforms they require become less expensive, many faculty are likely to develop software even without improvements in institutional support or rewards. In that belief, I share Robert Alun Jones's (1988) sense of the immediate present and not too distant future:

> In twenty years, when historians of technology write the chapter on hypermedia in higher education, they will most likely focus on two, seemingly inexplicable phenomena. The first will have been the initial reluctance of the vast majority of the professoriate, despite the availability and future promise of enormously powerful tools, to become even the least bit involved. The second will have been the way in which this inertia was broken through. (p. 44)

That breakthrough may occur in the area of English studies. Because knowledge making and meaning making are at the heart of English studies, hypermedia, with its radical redefinition of those processes, stands to impact English studies perhaps more than any other discipline in the academy. As that occurs, the ability to navigate electronic writing spaces, to use Bolter's (1991) term, will become transparent to functioning within the field. At that point, computers and writing merges with composition and disappears as a separate area of research and study. At that point, developing software becomes as common to writing instruction as the current preparation of traditional print classroom materials.

Revolutionary technologies are only revolutionary when they touch one's life. The "Age of Steam" meant nothing to an English farmer in some remote Yorkshire village until the day the railroad arrived and nothing was again the same. The English historian, E.J. Hobsbawm (1982), explains:

> It [the railroad] transformed the speed of movement—indeed of human life—from one measured in single miles per hour, and introduced the notion of a gigantic, nation-wide, complex and exact interlocking routine symbolized by the railway time-table (from which all subsequent "time-tables" took their name and inspiration). It revealed the possibilities of technical progress as nothing else had done, because it was both more advanced than most other forms of technical activity and omnipresent. (p. 110)

Like the Yorkshire farmer, anyone who writes cannot help but be touched by the new electronic technology, and when that becomes pervasive, the study and teaching of writing will be irrevocably changed. However, unlike the brute presence of industrial steel and steam, computer technology relies on the diminution of its physical presence and is mostly experienced through software, which is created through intellectual endeavor and imagination, the currency of academic life. Therefore, those of us who write, teach, and theorize about writing have a rare opportunity to play a part in our own destiny, to help shape the revolution.

Appendix

The following is a list of software programs mentioned in this book. The list provides a brief description of each program and, in some cases, a sample of the program interface.

Comments is a network-based writing response program (fig. 1). Writers can send a draft to a reader for response or a reader can request the draft of a writer. The program allows users to identify a section of text and append to it a comment. In addition, comments can be appended to comments, allowing multiple readers to offer input on a document. The networked nature of the program allows the writer to ask for clarification of comments and to establish a dialogue with readers.

CSILE (Computer-Supported Intentional Learning Environment) is a networked system that gives students simultaneous access to a database

---

Directions

Open the menus and choose one of the following from the *Options* menu card:

Send a Paper — to send a paper.

Request a Paper's Return — to request the return of a paper you have already sent.

Read a Paper — to read or make comments on a paper.

Delete Comments — to remove all comments from a paper.

Help — to call up the program's online help.

Report a Program Problem — to report a problem with the program.

Quit — to quit the Comments program.

Figure 1. The *Comments* program options. (Used by permission of the developer, Christine Neuwirth.)

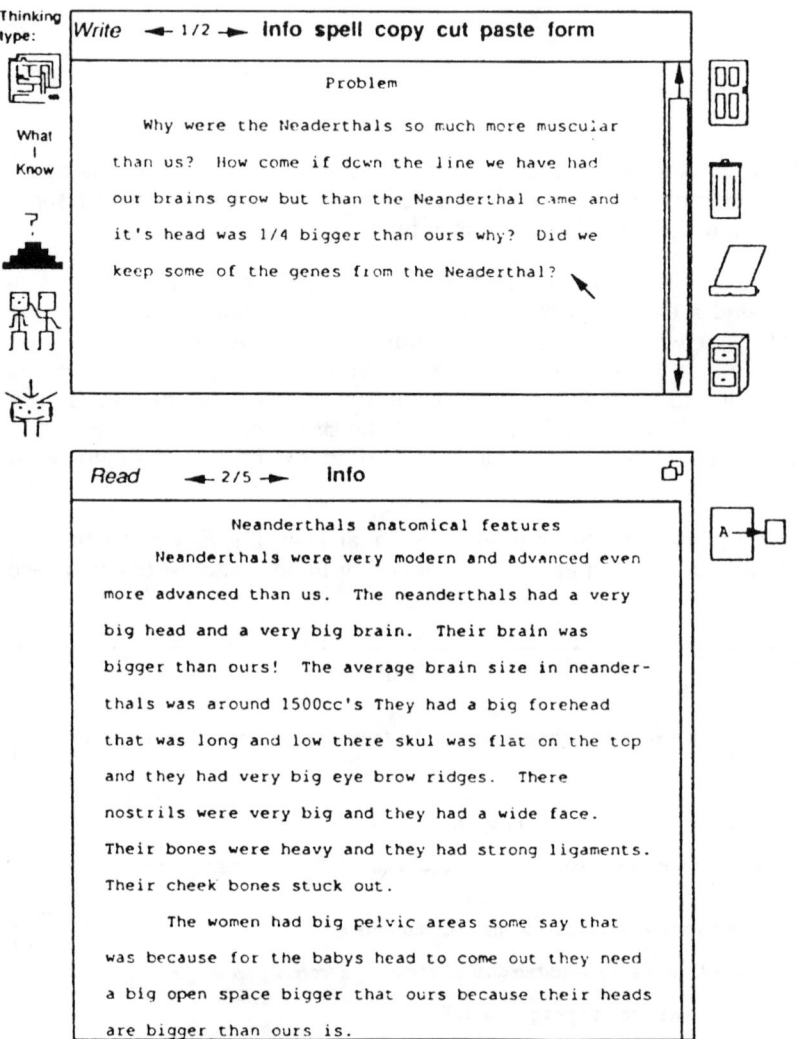

Figure 2. *CSILE* screen showing read-a-note and write-a-note windows. The arrows in a read-a-note window (top) permit stepping through a set of notes retrieved through a pseudonatural language Boolean search. The arrows on a write-a-note window (bottom) permit stepping through a set of notes in process. (Used by permission of the developer, Earl Woodruff.)

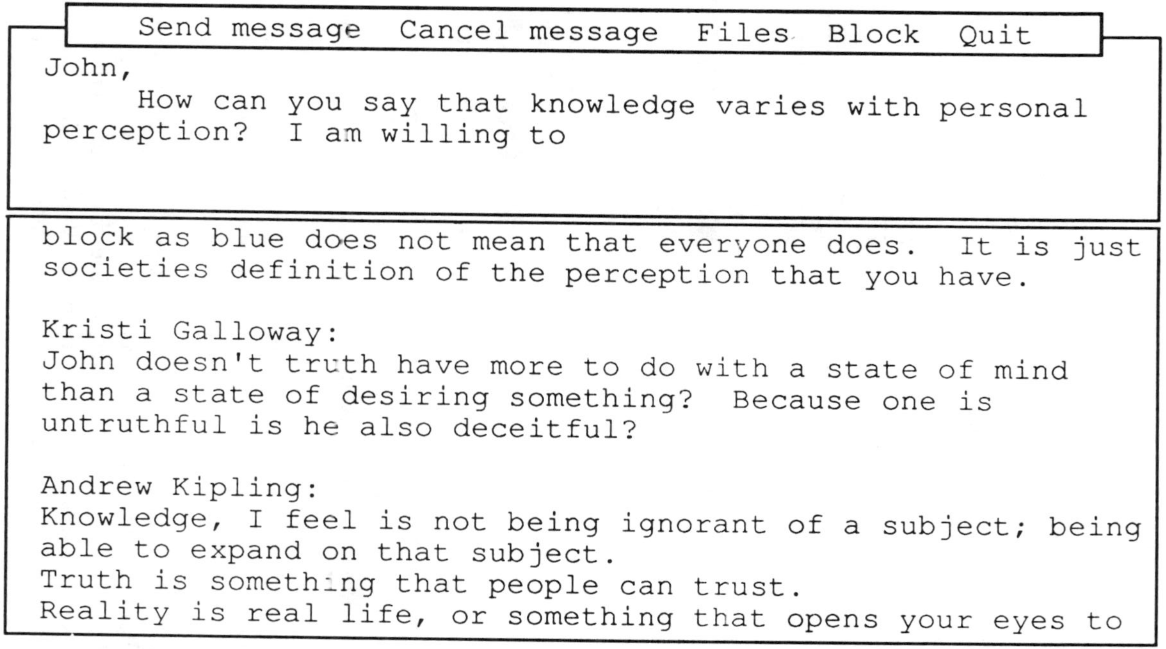

```
  Send message  Cancel message  Files  Block  Quit
```

John,
    How can you say that knowledge varies with personal
perception? I am willing to

---

block as blue does not mean that everyone does. It is just
societies definition of the perception that you have.

Kristi Galloway:
John doesn't truth have more to do with a state of mind
than a state of desiring something? Because one is
untruthful is he also deceitful?

Andrew Kipling:
Knowledge, I feel is not being ignorant of a subject; being
able to expand on that subject.
Truth is something that people can trust.
Reality is real life, or something that opens your eyes to

Figure 3. Sending a message in *Interchange*. When a conference participant wishes to send a message, an editing window pops up over the conference window. The individual can compose and edit a message before sending it out to become part of the public discussion. The active conversation remains partially visible in the bottom part of the screen. (Used by permission of the developer, Paul Taylor.)

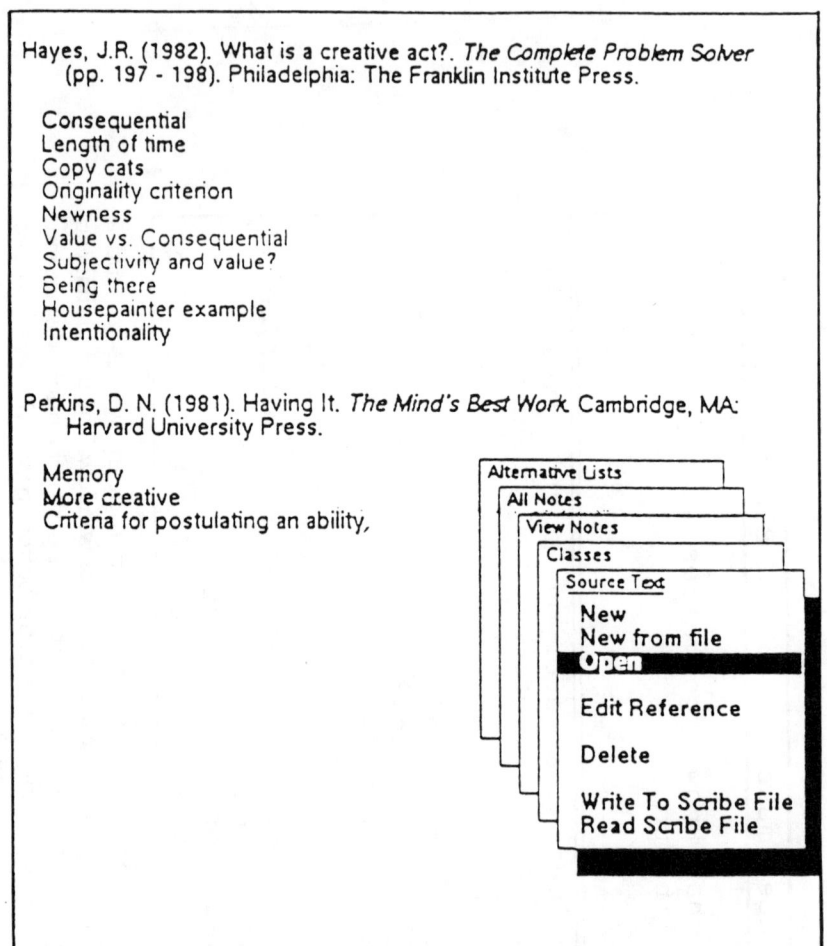

Figure 4. The *Notes* program window. (Used by permission of the developer, Christine Neuwirth.)

that is composed of text and graphical notes which the students produce themselves. The system provides students a means of searching and commenting on one another's contributions (fig. 2).

Interchange is a real-time or synchronous conferencing program that allows simultaneous text-based discussion in a networked computer classroom (fig. 3). The program allows on-line discussion, subconferences, and group analysis of text through a "View-a-File" function. *Interchange* is part of the *Daedalus Instructional System,* a set of

Appendix

integrated programs that include invention, e-mail, word processing, and revision, but each can be purchased separately.

Mindwriter is the invention program within the *Daedalus Instructional System*, though it can be purchased separately. The program is based on Hugh Burns's 1977 invention programs *TOPOI, TAGI,* and *BURKE*. *Mindwriter* offers three sets of prompts that are designed to help students explore a topic. As in Burns's *TOPOI* program, the prompt sets are based on Aristotle's *topoi*, Young, Becker, and Pike's tagmemics, and Burke's pentad.

Notes allows readers to make notes on on-line source texts and to make direct links between the source text and the electronically stored notes. The program maintains a list of all notes taken, and the user can then view selected notes, classify them, and organize them in various ways (fig. 4).

Organize is a prewriting program composed of modules for prewriting that include a large number of tutorials on development, generating ideas, audience assessment, creating an argument for debate, and approaches to drafting.

Prep Editor ("Work in Preparation") is a network-based program that supports collaborative writing, particularly through its co-authoring and commenting functions. The hypermedia capability of the program allows spatial representations of ideas and their restructuring. Authors can define "drafts," areas of that writing space which an author opens up to others for their collaboration and comments. The interface allows multiple on-screen "columns" that contain different types of information. For example, a set of columns might hold a draft, the larger outline into which it fits, and a reader's comments on that draft.

Prewrite is an invention program that prompts the user in brainstorming an expository essay or autobiographical/fictional work (fig. 5). The program prompts for information on topic, purpose, key ideas, audience, metaphor, and other components of the writing process. The answers can then be printed as a set of notes to be used in the first stage of the writing process. Instructors can modify the prompts.

Prose is an instructor feedback program that allows the user to respond within the student text with pre-programmed comments on mechanical errors (with built-in tutorials), the writer's own comments on any part of the text, or overall summary comments. *Prose* flags the text so that the responses are linked directly to the passage in question. In addition, the program allows the instructor to guide the revision by forcing the student to address the revisions in a given order.

SEEN offers six tutorials for examining or exploring a particular subject. The tutorials focus on character analysis, exploratory essays, art ex-

> **HI, what's your name?**
> Sandi Mackey
>
> **Any ideas on what to write? Y or N.**
> Yes, I want to write about soap operas and why so many people get hooked on them.
>
> **Okay. Now give me a one-to-five word title for your topic. Here are some examples: Feeling Blue, Are Schoolyards Safe?, Flying Saucers. What's your title?**
> Hooked on Soaps
>
> **What made you choose "Hooked on Soaps" to write about?**
> Because every afternoon the Student Center is filled with busy people watching General Hospital. And that includes me — even if I have a midterm and paper due the next day. Why do I do it? What's the lure? : . .

Figure 5. Excerpt from *Prewrite* questions. In *Prewrite*, a series of interactive questions and answers results in a printout of the writer's thoughts, which can be used as notes for developing a first draft. (Used by permission of the designer, Mimi Schwartz.)

ploration, historical conflicts, essay analysis, and plotting in literature. The tutorials can be customized by the instructor. The program also includes bulletin boards that allow for asynchronous collaboration among student writers.

Thoughtline was originally designed for business users who wanted help in the preparation of presentations or reports. It is an invention program that uses Artificial Intelligence (AI) features to prompt the user for information and then to refine or expand on that information.

The program creates an open-ended, nondirective dialogue with the user in the same manner of Joseph Weizenbaum's now famous *ELIZA* program.

WE is a hypertext "writing environment" program designed for a networked environment. Based on an explicit cognitive model of the writing process, *WE* operates within six distinct modes that can each operate in a separate window on screen. The user can quickly and easily move from one mode to another and manipulate screen objects which directly affect the text linked to those objects (in reorganizing the structure of an essay, for example).

Writer's Helper is a macro-environment program that offers a wide range of instructional modules or activities. These include nineteen prewriting activities that address discovery, invention, and organization, and twenty revising modules that address structure, audience, and style. The new *Windows* version of *Writer's Helper* includes more tools than the previous version and smoother integration with word-processing programs.

Works Cited

Allen, H.B. (1986). Facets: The joys and frustrations of writing textbooks. *English Journal, 75* (8), 12.

Anson, C.M. (1989). Computer deep cases for writing instruction. Paper presented at the Computers and Writing Conference. Minneapolis, Minnesota. May 13.

Balestri, D.P. (1988). Ivory towers, silicon basements: Learner-centered computing in postsecondary education. A report from the FIPSE Technology Study Group. McKinney, TX: Academic Computing Publications.

Barker, T.T., & Kemp, F.O. (1990). Network theory: A postmodern pedagogy for the writing classroom. In C. Handa (Ed.), *Computers and community: Teaching composition in the twenty-first century* (pp. 1–27). Portsmouth, NH: Boynton-Cook.

Batson, T. (1988). The ENFI project: A networked classroom approach to writing instruction. *Academic Computing, 2* (2), 32–57.

Beaugrande, R., de. (1985). Composition textbooks: Ethnography and proposal. *Written Communication, 2,* 391–413.

Beck, R.J., & Spicer, D. (1988). Hypermedia in academia. *Academic Computing, 2* (2), 22–30.

Beesley, M.S. (1986). The effects of word processing on elementary students' written compositions: Processes, products, and attitudes. Ph.D. diss. Indiana University at Bloomington. *DAI, 47* (4006A).

Bereiter, C., & Scardamalia, M. (1983). Levels of inquiry in writing research. In P. Mosenthal, L. Tamor, & S.A. Walmsley (Eds.), *Research on writing: Principles and methods* (pp. 3–25). New York: Longman.

Berlin, J.A. (1987). *Rhetoric and reality: Writing instruction in American colleges, 1900–1985.* Carbondale: Southern Illinois University Press.

Berlin, J.A. (1988). Rhetoric and ideology in the writing class. *College English, 50,* 477–494.

Bernstein, M. (1988). Hypertext: New challenges and roles for technical communicators. *Proceedings of the 35th International Technical Communication Conference.* ATA33–ATA36. Society for Technical Communication.

Bizzell, P. (1982). Cognition, convention, and certainty: What we need to know about writing. *Pre/Text, 3,* 213–243.

Boden, M.A. (1977). *Artificial intelligence and natural man.* New York: Basic Books.

Bolter, J.D. (1984). *Turing's man: Western culture in the computer age.* Chapel Hill: University of North Carolina Press.

Bolter, J.D. (1991). *Writing space: The computer, hypertext, and the history of writing.* Hillsdale: Lawrence Earlbaum.

Bourque, J.H. (1983). Understanding and evaluating: The humanist as a computer specialist. *College English, 45,* 67–73.

Bruffee, K.A. (1983). Writing and reading as collaborative or social acts: The argument from Kuhn and Vygotsky. In J.N. Hays, P.A. Roth, J.R. Ramsey, & R.D. Foulke (Eds.), *The writer's mind: Writing as a mode of thinking* (pp. 159–169). Urbana: National Council of Teachers of English.

Burnett, J.H. (1984). Word processing as a writing tool of an elementary school student: A single case experiment with nine replications. Ph.D. diss. University of Maryland. *DAI, 47* (1183A).

Burns, D. (1987). *Thoughtline* software: A computer to help you write a speech. *Executive Communications, 8,* 5.

Burns, D. (1989). Telephone interview. February 20.

Burns, H.L. (1980). Simulating invention in English composition through computer-assisted instruction. *Educational Technology, 20,* 5–10.

Burns, H.L. (1984). The challenge for computer-assisted rhetoric. *Computers and the Humanities, 18,* 173–181.

Burns, H.L. (1988). Personal interview. San Antonio, Texas. August 29.

Burns, H.L., & Capps, C.G. (1988). Foundations of intelligent tutoring systems: An introduction. In M.C. Polson & J.J. Richardson (Eds.), *Foundations of intelligent tutoring systems* (pp. 1–19). Hillsdale, NJ: Lawrence Erlbaum.

Butler, W. (1991). Personal interview. Seattle, Washington. November.

Carbonell, J.R. (1970). AI in CAI: An artificial intelligence approach to computer-aided instruction. *IEEE Transactions on Man-Machine Systems, 11,* 190–202.

Works Cited

Cardwell, D.S.L. (1972). *Turning points in western technology: A study of technology, science, and history.* New York: Neale Watson Academic Publications.

Carlson, P. (1988). Hypertext: A way of incorporating user feedback into online documentation. In E. Barrett (Ed.), *Text, context, and hypertext: Writing with and for the computer* (pp. 93–110). Cambridge, MA: Massachusetts Institute of Technology Press.

Carter, L. (1988). Personal interview. Austin, Texas. August 29.

Catano, J.V. (1985). Computer-based writing: Navigating the fluid text. *College Composition and Communication, 36,* 309–316.

Cavalier, R., & Friend, K.E. (1988). Educational software frontiers. In Sprecher, J.W. (Ed.), *Facilitating academic software development* (pp. 99–120). McKinney, TX: Academic Computing Publications.

Chambers, J.A., & Lewis, D.O. (1988). The effects of academic software on learning and motivation. In Sprecher, J.W. (Ed.), *Facilitating academic software development* (pp. 71–98). McKinney, TX: Academic Computing Publications.

Cirello, V.J. (1986). The effect of word processing on the writing abilities of tenth-grade remedial writing students. Ph.D. diss. New York University. *DAI, 47* (2531A).

Clark, Suzanne. (1989). Feminism, poststructuralism, and rhetoric: If we change language, do we also change the world? Paper presented at the Conference on College Composition and Communication. Seattle, Washington. March 17.

Collier, R. (1983). The word processor and revision strategies. *College Composition and Communication, 34,* 149–155.

Collier, R., Gerand, H., Parbs, R., & Morrison, P. (1987). Computer writing facilities: The state of the art. Report to the English Department, Mount Royal College, Calgary, Alberta, Canada. June.

Connors, R.J. (1986). Textbooks and the evolution of the discipline. *College Composition and Communication, 37,* 178–194.

Coulter, C.A. (1986). Writing with word processors: Effects on cognitive development, revision, and writing quality. Ph.D. diss. University of Oklahoma. *DAI, 47* (2551A).

Coursey, D. (1988). Revised *Thoughtline* package is writers' tool. *MIS Week,* July 4, 1.

Curley, W.P., & Strickland, J. (1986). Garbage in/garbage out: Evaluating computer software. *The English Record, 37,* 11–14.

Curtis, M. (1988). When writing is revision: Teaching revision on the word processor. *College Composition and Communication, 39,* 337–344.

Daiute, C. (1985). *Writing and computers.* Reading, MA: Addison-Wesley.

Daiute, C. (1986). Physical and cognitive factors in revising: Insights from studies with computers. *Research in the Teaching of English, 20,* 141–159.

Dalton, D.W., & Hannafin, M.J. (1987). The effects of word processing on written composition. *Journal of Educational Research, 80,* 338–342.

Debs, M.B. (1989). A different collaboration: Word processing and the workplace. Paper presented at the Conference on College Composition and Communication. Seattle, Washington. March 17.

Dinan, J.S., Gagnon, R., & Taylor, J. (1986). Integrating computers into the writing classroom: Some guidelines. *Computers and Composition, 3,* 33–39.

DiPardo, A., & DiPardo, M. (1989). Toward the metapersonal essay: Exploring the potential of hypertext in the composition classroom. Paper presented at the Computers and Writing Conference. Minneapolis, Minnesota. May 13.

Doheny-Farina, S., & Odell, L. (1985). Ethnographic research on writing: Assumptions and methodology. In L. Odell & D. Goswami (Eds.), *Writing in nonacademic settings* (pp. 503–525). New York: Guilford Press.

Dreyfus, H. (1979). *What computers can't do: The limits of artificial intelligence.* Rev. ed. New York: Harper & Row.

Duling, R.A. (1985). Word processors and student writing: A study of their impact on revision, fluency, and quality of writing. Ph.D. diss. Michigan State University. *DAI, 46* (1823A).

Edwards, J. (1987). AI-based outliner tackles writer's block. *PC Week,* June 2, 1.

Eisenstein, E.L. (1979). *The printing press as an agent of change: Communications and cultural transformations in early modern Europe.* New York: Cambridge University Press.

Elbow, P. (1973). *Writing without teachers.* New York: Oxford University Press.

Elbow, P. (1990). *What Is English?* New York: Modern Language Association.

Works Cited

Eldred, J.M. (1989). Computers, composition pedagogy, and the social view. In G.E. Hawisher & C.L. Selfe (Eds.), *Critical perspectives on computers and composition instruction* (pp. 201–218). New York: Teachers College Press.

Eldred, J.M., & Fortune, R. (1992). Exploring the implications of metaphors for computer networks and hypermedia. In G.E. Hawisher & P.J. LeBlanc (Eds.), *Re-Imagining computers and composition: Teaching and research in the virtual age* (pp. 58–73). Portsmouth, NH: Boynton/Cook.

Faigley, L. (1986). Competing theories of process: A critique and proposal. *College English, 48,* 527–542.

Fersko-Weiss, H. (1991). 3D reading with the hypertext edge. *PC, 10,* 240–261.

Fish, S.E. (1980). *Is there a text in this class? The authority of interpretive communities.* Cambridge, MA: Harvard University Press.

Flower, L. (1989). Cognition, context, and theory building. *College Composition and Communication, 40,* 282–311.

Flower, L., & Hayes, J.R. (1981). A cognitive process theory of writing. *College Composition and Communication, 32,* 365–387.

Flynn, L. (1989). HyperCard-like programs confuse the DOS market. *InfoWorld,* June 12, 21.

Fortune, R. (1991). Personal interview. Seattle, Washington. November 23.

Giroux, H.A. (1983). *Theory and resistance in education: A pedagogy for the opposition.* S. Hadley, MA: Bergin & Garvey.

Goetz, J.P., & LeCompte, M.D. (1981). Ethnographic research and the problem of data reduction. *Anthropology and Education Quarterly, 7,* 51–70.

Grabowski, B., Suciati, I., & Pusch, W. (1990). Social and intellectual value of computer-mediated communications in a graduate community. *Educational Training and Technology International, 27,* 276–283.

Graves, R.L. (Ed.). (1984). *Rhetoric and composition: A sourcebook for teachers and writers.* Rev. 2nd ed. Portsmouth, NH: Boynton/Cook.

Gumpert, G., & Cathcart, R. (1985). Media grammars, generations, and media gaps. *Critical Studies in Mass Communications, 2,* 23–35.

Haas, C. (1989). Seeing it on the screen isn't really seeing it: Computer writers' reading problems. In G.E. Hawisher & C.L. Selfe (Eds.), *Critical perspectives on computers and composition instruction* (pp. 44–69). New York: Teachers College Press.

Haas, C., & Hayes, J.R. (1986). What did I just say? Reading problems in writing with the machine. *Research in the Teaching of English, 20,* 22–35.

Hairston, M. (1982). The winds of change: Thomas Kuhn and the revolution in the teaching of writing. *College Composition and Communication, 33,* 78–86.

Hairston, M. (1985). Breaking our bounds and reaffirming our connections. *College Composition and Communication, 36,* 272–282.

Hale, D.G. (1984). Word processing: Panacea or problem? *English Record, 35,* 10–11.

Halpern, J.W. (1985). An electronic odyssey. In L. Odell & D. Goswami (Eds.), *Writing in non-academic settings* (pp. 157–202). New York: Guilford Press.

Halpern, J.W., & Liggett, S. (1984). *Computers and composing: How the new technologies are changing writing.* Carbondale: Southern Illinois University Press.

Hammersley, M., & Atkinson, P. (1983). *Ethnography: Principles in practice.* London: Tavistock.

Harris, J. (1985). Student writers and word processing: A preliminary evaluation. *College Composition and Communication, 36,* 323–330.

Havelock, E.A. (1982). *The literate revolution in Greece and its cultural consequences.* Princeton, NJ: Princeton University Press.

Hawisher, G.E. (1989). Research and recommendations for computers and composition. In G.E. Hawisher & C.L. Selfe (Eds.), *Critical perspectives on computers and instruction* (pp. 44–69). New York: Teachers College Press.

Hawkins, B. (1989). Campus-wide networking at Brown University. *Academic Computing, 3,* 32–49.

Hepler, M. (1992). Telephone interview. February 6.

Herrmann, A. (1989). Computers in public schools: Are we being realistic? In G.E. Hawisher & C.L. Selfe (Eds.), *Critical perspectives on computers and composition instruction* (pp. 109–143). New York: Teachers College Press.

Hiltz, S.R. (1988). Collaborative learning in a virtual classroom: Highlights of findings. Paper presented at the Computer Supported Cooperative Work Conference. June.

Hobsbawm, E.J. (1982). *Industry and empire: From 1750 to the present.* 3rd ed. Hammondsworth: Penguin.

Johnson, G. (1987). *Machinery of the mind: Inside the new science of artificial intelligence.* Redmon, WA: Tempus.

Johnson-Laird, P. (1983). *Mental models: Toward a cognitive science of language, inference, and consciousness.* Cambridge, MA: Harvard University Press.

Johnston, S.J. (1989). Software reusability depends on teamwork and cooperation. *InfoWorld*, June 19, 19.

Jones, R.A. (1988). Building a hypermedia laboratory. *Academic Computing*, 2 (10), 24–44.

Kantor, K., Kirby, D., & Goetz, J.P. (1981). Research in context: Ethnographic studies in English education. *Research in the Teaching of English*, 15, 293–309.

Kaplan, H. (1986). Computers and composition: Improving students' written performance. Ph.D. diss. University of Massachusetts at Amherst. *DAI*, 47 (776A).

Kaplan, N. (1989). Telephone interview. February 1.

Kaplan, N. (1991a). Ideology, technology, and the future of writing instruction. In G.E. Hawisher & C.L. Selfe (Eds.), *Evolving perspectives on computers and composition studies: Questions for the 1990s* (pp.11–42). Urbana: National Council of Teachers of English/Computers and Composition.

Kaplan, N. (1991b). Telephone interview. December 8.

Kaufer, D.A. (1989). Designing and implementing of a computer-supported writing curriculum: Theory and practice. Paper presented at the Computers and Writing Conference. Minneapolis, Minnesota. May 13.

Keane, D., & Gaither, G. (1988). The effects of academic software on learning and motivation. In J.W. Sprecher (Ed.), *Facilitating Academic Software Development* (pp. 47–69). McKinney, TX: Academic Computing Publications.

Kemp, F. (1988). Personal interview. Austin, Texas. August 29.

Kemp, F. (1989). Telephone interview. February 2.

Kemp, F. (1991). Telephone interview. December 5.

Landow, G.P., & Delaney, P. (Eds.). (1991). *Hypermedia and literary studies*. Cambridge, MA: Massachusetts Institute of Technology Press.

Lanham, R. (1989). The electronic word: Literary study and the digital revolution. In *New Literary History, 20,* 265–290.

Larson, R.L. (1989). Review of *The making of knowledge in composition: Portrait of an emerging field. College English, 40,* 95–98.

Laub, L. (1986). The evolution of mass storage. *Byte, 2,* 161–172.

LeBlanc, P.J. (1988). How to get the words just right: A reappraisal of word processing and revision. *Computers and Composition, 5,* 29–42.

LeBlanc, P.J. (1992). Ringing in the virtual age: Hypermedia authoring software and the revival of faculty-based software development in composition. In G.E. Hawisher & P.J. LeBlanc (Eds.), *Re-Imagining computers and composition: Teaching and research in the virtual age* (pp. 191–206). Portsmouth, NH: Boynton/Cook.

LeBlanc, P., & Moran, C. (1989). Adapting to a new environment: Word processing and the training of writing teachers. In C.L. Selfe, D. Rodrigues, & W.R. Oates (Eds.), *Computers in English and language arts: The challenge of teacher education* (pp. 111–130). Urbana: National Council of Teachers of English.

LeCompte, M.D., & Goetz, J.P. (1982). Problems of reliability and validity in ethnographic research. *Review of Educational Research, 52,* 31–60.

Lewis, P.H. (1992). The computer as catalyst. *New York Times Educational Supplement,* January 5, 48–50.

Lloyd-Jones, R. (1989). Review of *The making of knowledge in composition: Portrait of an emerging field. College English, 40,* 98–100.

Lunsford, A.A. (1991). Conditions for literacy. Paper presented at the Modern Language Association Convention. Seattle, Washington.

McCreary, E. (1989). Computer-mediated communication and organizational culture. In R. Mason & A. Kaye (Eds.), *Mindweave: Communication, computers, and distance education* (pp. 101–112). New York: Pergamon Press.

McDaid, J. (1989). Breaking frames: Toward an ecology of hypermedia. Paper presented at the Computers and Writing Conference. Minneapolis, Minnesota. May 13.

McDaid, J. (1991). Toward an ecology of hypermedia. In G.E. Hawisher & C.L. Selfe (Eds.), *Evolving perspectives on computers and composition studies: Questions for the 1990s* (pp. 203–223). Urbana: National Council of Teachers of English/*Computers and Composition.*

McDaniel, E. (1987). Bibliography of text-analysis and writing-instruction software. *Journal of Advanced Composition, 7,* 139–169.

McKenzie, A.T. (1991). The academic on-line. In *Profession 91* (pp. 41–48). New York: Modern Language Association.

McLuhan, M. (1962). *The Gutenberg galaxy: The making of typographic man.* Toronto: University of Toronto Press.

Madigan, C. (1984). The tools that shape us: Composing by hand vs. composing by machine. *English Education, 16,* 143–149.

Manzelli, J. (1991). Telephone interview. November 18.

Marcus, S. (1983). Real-time gadgets with feedback: Special effects in computer-assisted instruction. *The Writing Instructor, 2,* 174–181.

Marcus, S., & Blau, S. (1983). Not seeing is believing: Invisible writing with computers. *Educational Technology, 23,* 12–15.

Meeker, M. (1986). Waiting for WANDAH: A critique of present trends in computer-assisted composition. *Computer-Assisted Composition Journal, 1,* 42–54.

MicroSelect: The essential tool. (1986). Marketing materials distributed by Robotel Electronique, Inc. Montreal, Quebec, Canada.

Minsky, M. (1981). A framework for representing knowledge. In J. Haugeland (Ed.), *Mind design: Philosophy, psychology, artificial intelligence* (pp. 95–128). Cambridge, MA: Massachusetts Institute of Technology Press.

Moore, M.A. (1987). The effect of word processing technology in a developmental writing program on writing quality, attitude toward composing, and revision strategies of fourth- and fifth-grade students. Ph.D. diss. University of South Florida. *DAI, 48* (635A).

Moran, C. (1983). Word-processing and the teaching of writing. *English Journal, 72,* (3) 113–115.

Moran, C. (1984). The word-processor and the writer. *Computers and Composition, 2,* 1–5.

Moran, C. (1991). Teaching writing in the virtual classroom: Good news and bad. Paper presented at the Modern Language Association Convention. San Francisco, California. December.

Moran, C. (1992). Computers and the writing classroom: A look to the future. In G.E. Hawisher & P.J. LeBlanc (Eds.), *Re-Imagining computers and composition: Teaching and research in the virtual age* (pp. 7–23). Portsmouth, NH: Boynton/Cook.

Morgan, B.A. (1985). Evaluating student papers with a word processor. *Collegiate Microcomputer, 3,* 345–350.

Moulthrop, S. (1991). The politics of hypertext. In G.E. Hawisher & C.L. Selfe (Eds.), *Evolving perspectives on computers and composition studies: Questions for the 1990s* (pp. 253–271). Urbana: National Council of Teachers of English/Computers and Composition.

Mumford, L. (1934). Technics and civilization. New York: Harcourt Brace.

Murray, D. (1985). Composition as conversation: The computer terminal as medium of conversation. In L. Odell & D. Goswami (Eds.), *Writing in non-academic settings* (pp. 203–228). New York: Guilford Press.

Nadel, S.F. (1976). The interview technique in social anthropology. In F.C. Bartlett, M. Ginsberg, E.J. Lindgren, & R.H. Thouless (Eds.), *The study of society: Methods and problems* (pp. 317–328). London: Routledge and Kegan Paul.

Nelson, T. (1987). *Literary machines: The report on, and of, Project Xanadu concerning word processing, electronic publishing, hypertext, tinkertoys, tomorrow's intellectual revolution, and education and freedom.* Ed. 87.1. Swarthmore, PA: Theodor H. Nelson.

Nelson, T. (1988). The call of the ocean: Hypertext universal and open. *Hyper Age,* May/June, 5–7.

Neuwirth, C. (1989a). Telephone interview. March 6.

Neuwirth, C. (1989b). Creating the dialogue: Using the network to initiate collaborative learning and writing. Paper presented at the Computers and Writing Conference. Minneapolis, Minnesota. May 13.

Neuwirth, C. (1991). Telephone interview. December 9.

Newell, A., Shaw, J.C., & Simon, H.A. (1957). Empirical explorations of the logic theory machine: A case study in heuristics. Report P-951. The Rand Corporation. March.

Newman, J. (1987). On-line: Using a database in the classroom. *Language Arts, 63,* 315–319.

Ney, J.W. (1986). Facets: The joys and frustrations of writing textbooks. *English Journal, 75* (8), 12.

North, S.M. (1987). *The making of knowledge in composition: Portrait of an emerging field.* Upper Montclair, NJ: Boynton/Cook.

Odell, L., Goswami, D., Herrington, A., & Quick, D. (1983). Studying writing in non-academic settings. In P.V. Anderson, R.J. Brockman, & C.R. Miller (Eds.), *New essays in technical and scientific communication: Research, theory, and practice* (pp. 17–40). Farmingdale, NY: Baywood.

Ohmann, R. (1985). Literacy, technology, and monopoly capital. *College English, 47,* 675–689.

Ong, W.J., S.J. (1982). *Orality and literacy: The technologizing of the world.* New York: Methuen.

Palmquist, M. (1989). Extending the dialogue: Using the network to evaluate and support student writing. Paper presented at the Computers and Writing Conference. Minneapolis, Minnesota. May 13.

Parlett, J. (1987). *Confer: An ICAI system for prewriting and reflective inquiry.* Ph.D. diss. University of Pittsburgh. *DAI, 49* (05A).

Parlett, J. (1989). Personal interview. Minneapolis, Minnesota. May 13.

Polson, M.C., & Richardson, J.J. (Eds.). (1988). *Foundations of intelligent tutoring systems.* Hillsdale, NJ: Lawrence Erlbaum. "Put stars in your head." (1987). *Washington Post,* July 10, C5.

Raymond, J.C. (1989). Review of *The making of knowledge in composition: Portrait of an emerging field. College English, 40,* 93–95.

Richardson, K. (1992). Telephone interview. February 10.

Ringle, M. (Ed.). (1979). *Philosophical perspectives in artificial intelligence.* Atlantic Highlands, NJ: Humanities Press.

Rodrigues, D., & Rodrigues, R.J. (1984). Computer-based invention: Its place and potential. *College Composition and Communciation, 35,* 78–87.

Romiszowski, A. (1990). Shifting paradigms in education and training: What is the connection with telecommunications? *Educational and Training Technology International, 27,* 233–236.

Rosenthal, J.W. (1987). Integrating word processing into freshman composition. *Computer-Assisted Composition Journal, 1,* 119–131.

Ross, D. (1989). Beyond NeXt. Paper presented at the Computers and Writing Conference. Minneapolis, Minnesota. May 13.

Schwartz, H. (1990). Ethical considerations of ethical computer use. In D.H. Holdstein & C.L. Selfe (Eds.), *Computers and writing: Theory, research, practice* (pp. 18–30). New York: Modern Language Association.

Schwartz, H. (1992). Telephone interview. February 4.

Schwartz, M. (1985). *Writing for many roles*. Upper Montclair, NJ: Boynton/Cook.

Schwartz, M. (1989). Telephone interview. February 2.

Schwartz, M. (1992). Telephone interview. February 4.

Schwartz, M. (Forthcoming). *Swimming above the black line*.

Schwartz, M. (Ed.). (1991). *Writer's craft, teacher's art: Teaching what we know*. Portsmouth, NH: Heinemann.

Selfe, C.L. (1985). *Computer-assisted instruction in composition: Create your own*. Urbana: National Council of Teachers of English.

Selfe, C.L. (1989a). Personal interview. Seattle, Washington. March 18.

Selfe, C.L. (1989b). An open letter to computer colleagues: Notes from the margin. Paper presented at the Conference on Computers and Writing. Minneapolis, Minnesota. May 13.

Selfe, C.L. (1989c). Redefining literacy: The multilayered grammars of computers. In G.E. Hawisher & C.L. Selfe (Eds.), *Critical perspectives on computers and composition instruction* (pp. 3–15). New York: Teachers College Press.

Selfe, C.L. (1990). Technology in the English classroom: Computers through the lens of feminist theory. In C. Handa (Ed.), *Computers and community: Teaching composition in the twenty-first century* (pp. 118–139). Portsmouth, NH: Boynton/Cook.

Selfe, C.L. (1992). Preparing English teachers for the virtual age: The case for technology critics. In G.E. Hawisher & P.J. LeBlanc (Eds.), *Re-Imagining computers and composition: Teaching and research in the virtual age* (pp. 24–42). Portsmouth, NH: Boynton/Cook.

Shirk, H.N. (1985). Hyperrhetoric: Teaching students to develop hypertext discourse models. Paper presented at the Computers and Writing Conference. Minneapolis, Minnesota. May 13.

Shirk, H.N. (1991). Hypertext and composition studies. In G.E. Hawisher & C.L. Selfe (Eds.), *Evolving perspectives on computers and composition studies: Questions for the 1990s* (pp. 177–202). Urbana: National Council of Teachers of English/Computers and Composition.

Shor, I. (1987). *Critical teaching and everyday life*. Chicago: University of Chicago Press.

Shriner, D.K. (1988). Risk taking, revising, and word processing. *Computers and Composition, 5*, 43–54.

Simon, J.F. (1989). A user-friendly revolution: Object orientation may point the way. *Boston Globe,* May 21, A1.

Slatin, J. (1990). Reading hypertext: Order and coherence in a new medium. *College English, 52,* 870–883.

Sledd, A. (1988). Readin' not riotin': The politics of literacy. *College English, 50,* 495–508.

Smith, C.F. (1989). Reconsidering hypertext. Paper presented at the Computers and Writing Conference. Minneapolis, Minnesota. May 13.

Smith, C.F. (1991). Reconceiving hypertext. In G.E. Hawisher & C.L. Selfe (Eds.), *Evolving perspectives on computers and composition studies: Questions for the 1990s* (pp. 224–252). Urbana: National Council of Teachers of English/*Computers and Composition.*

Smith, J.B. (1989). Personal interview. Minneapolis, Minnesota. May 13.

Smith, J.B., & Lansman, M. (1987). A cognitive basis for a computer writing environment. TextLab Report #TR87-032. University of North Carolina at Chapel Hill. June.

Smith, J.B., Weiss, S.F., & Ferguson, G.J. (1987). A hypertext environment and its cognitive basis. TextLab Report #TR87-033. University of North Carolina at Chapel Hill. October.

Spitzer, M. (1986). Writing style in computer conferences. In V. Arms (Ed.), *IEEE Transactions on Professional Communication: Special Issue on Computer Conferencing* (pp. 19–22).

Sprecher, J.W. (1988). The future of software development in higher education. In J.W. Sprecher (Ed.), *Facilitating academic software development* (pp. 121–156). McKinney, TX: Academic Computing Publications.

Stewart, D.C. (1978). Composition textbooks and the assault on tradition. *College Composition and Communication, 29,* 171–176.

Strassman, P.A. (1983). Information systems and literacy. In R.W. Bailey & R.M. Fosheim (Eds.), *Literacy for life: The demand for reading and writing* (pp. 115–121). New York: Modern Language Association.

Strickland, J. (1988). Telephone interview. September 14.

Sudol, R. (1985). Applied word processing: Notes on authority, responsibility, and revision in a workshop model. *College Composition and Communication, 36,* 331–335.

Tamplin, J., & Adams, C. (1986). Word-processing: Does it work? *Electronic Education, 5,* 101–116.

Taylor, P. (1989a). Telephone interview. January 30.

Taylor, P. (1989b). Personal interview. Austin, Texas. August 29.

Thiesmeyer, J. (1984). Some boundary considerations for writing software. In L.S. Bridwell & D. Ross (Eds.), *Computers and composition: Selected papers* (pp. 277–291). Fort Collins: Colorado State University/Michigan Technological University.

Townsend, C. (1988). *Understanding C.* Indianapolis: Howard W. Sams.

Trimbur, J. (1989). Consensus and difference in collaborative learning. *College English, 51,* 602–616.

Tuman, M. (1989). 'Caverns measureless to man': The prospects for post-typographical literacy. Paper presented at the Computers and Writing Conference. Minneapolis, Minnesota. May 13.

Turing, A.M. (1937). On computable numbers, with an application to the *entscheidungsproblem.* In *Proceedings of the London Mathematics Society,* 2nd ser. 42, 230–265. London: C.F. Hodgson.

Turing, A.M. (1964). Computing machinery and intelligence. Rpt. in A.R. Anderson (Ed.), *Minds and machines* (pp. 4–30). Englewood Cliffs, NJ: Prentice-Hall.

Warwick, D.P., & Lininger, C.A. (1975). *The sample survey: Theory and practice.* New York: McGraw-Hill.

Weizenbaum, J. (1965). *ELIZA:* A computer program for the study of natural language communication between man and machine. *Communications of the Association for Computing Machinery, 9,* 36–45.

Weizenbaum, J. (1976). *Computer power and human reason: From judgement to calculation.* San Francisco: W.H. Freeman.

Welch, K.E. (1987). Ideology and freshman textbook production: The place of theory in writing pedagogy. *College Composition and Communication, 38,* 269–282.

Winograd, T., & Flores, F. (1986). *Understanding computers and cognition: A new foundation for design.* Norwood, NJ: Ablex.

Winterowd, W.R. (1989). Composition textbooks: Publisher-author relationships. *College Composition and Communication, 40,* 139–151.

Witte, S. (1983). Topical structure and revision. *College Composition and Communication, 34,* 313–341.

Woodruff, E. (1989). Telephone interview. March 13.

Woolley, W.C. (1985). The effects of word processing on the writing of selected fifth-grade students. Ph.D. diss. College of William and Mary. *DAI, 47* (82A).

Wresch, W. (1992). Telephone interview. January 29.

Young, R. (1978). Paradigms and problems: Needed research in rhetorical invention. In C.R. Cooper & L. Odell (Eds.), *Research on composing: Points of departure* (pp. 29–48). Urbana: National Council of Teachers of English.

Zimmerman, M. (1989). Reconstruction of a profession: New roles for writers in the computer industry. In E. Barrett (Ed.), *The society of text: Hypertext, hypermedia, and the social construction of information* (pp. 35–49). Cambridge, MA: Massachusetts Institute of Technology Press.

Zinsser, W. (1983). *Writing with a word processor.* New York: Harper & Row.

Author

Paul J. LeBlanc is associate professor of English and chair of the humanities department at Springfield College. His publications include *Re-Imagining Computers and Composition: Research and Teaching in the Virtual Age* (edited with Gale E. Hawisher), chapters on the politics of technology in secondary schools in *Literacy and Computers* (edited by Cynthia L. Selfe and Susan Hilligos), on hypertext in a forthcoming volume on hypertext and software development (edited by William Condon), and on teacher training and computers (with Charles Moran) in *Computers in English and the Language Arts: The Challenge of Teacher Education* (edited by Cynthia L. Selfe, Dawn Rodrigues, and William Oates). His articles have appeared in *Thalia, SIGCUE Outlook,* and *Computers and Composition.* He has presented at NCTE, CCCC, MLA, New Hampshire Conference on Composition, and various educational and corporate organizations. He is currently software editor for *Computers and Composition* and serves on the software subcommittee of NCTE's Instructional Technology Committee.

Index

Academic Computing, 53
Academic Software Development Survey (EDUCOM), 41, 52, 87–88, 96, 99
Academic work vs. software work, 116–117, 121–122, 123
Air Force, 16, 133
ANDREW (network system), 141
Anson, Chris M., 110
Apple Computer, Inc.
   academic collaboration with, 132
   funding from, 40, 97, 131
   in future of CAC, 110
   Macintosh computers, 76–77, 82, 100, 110
   software for computers by, 25, 32, 73
   system architecture by, 79
Architecture, system. *See* System architecture
Arms, Valerie, 34
Army Research Institute, 64, 133
Artificial intelligence, 82–87
Asymetrix Corporation, 71, 111
Atkinson, Bill, 73
Augmented transition network (ATN), 83

B., Rich, 132
Babbage, Charles, 13
Bajarin, Tim, 111
Balister, Valerie, 46
Barker, Thomas T., 126, 128
Barthes, Roland, 126
BASIC (programming language), 25
Batson, Trent, 46, 47, 80, 126
Beck, J. Robert, 73, 75–76
Beesley, M. S., 6
Bentham, Jeremy, 130
Bereiter, C., 58, 136, 139, 140
Berlin, James A., 66
Bolter, J. David, 18, 126, 150

Bourque, Joseph H., 12, 90–91, 95
BreadNet, 81
BRUNET (Brown University network), 82
Bump, Jerome, 44, 45
Burnett, J. H., 6
Burns, Dan, 25, 52, 53–56, 82, 83, 115
Burns, Hugh, 6, 26, 42, 44, 45, 83, 85. *See also* Daedalus Group
Business Week, 54
Butler, Wayne
   on academics vs. software design, 117
   on future of CAC, 115–116
   on reward and recognition, 88
   in software development, 42, 45–46, 49, 51, 52, 66
   See also Daedalus Group

C (programming language), 25, 103
C++ (programming language), 25
CAC (Computer-Aided Composition)
   composition theory in, 89, 93–94
   difficulties in development of, 12, 120
   evaluation of, 91–92, 149
   future of, in general, 146–151
   humanistic vs. technological perspectives in, 94–96
   writing environments in, 109–110, 118–119, 140–141
   See also Cognitive software models; Design/development, of software; Programming; *names of specific software*
California State University, 96
Carnegie Mellon University, 57, 59–61, 64–65, 97, 133, 142–143, 144

Carter, Locke, 42, 45, 47. *See also* Daedalus Group
CCCC (Conference on College Composition and Communication), 45, 46, 115
CCCC Bibliography of Composition and Rhetoric, 149
CD-ROM technology, 81–82
CD-RW (Compact Disc-Read Write) drives, 82
CD-WORM (Compact Disc-Write Once, Read Many) drives, 82
Center for Applied Cognitive Science, 57, 59, 64
"Challenge for Computer-Assisted Rhetoric" (H. Burns), 85
Chambers, Jack A., 22, 42
Cirello, V. J., 6
Clark, Suzanne, 94
"Cognitive Basis for a Computer Writing Environment, A" (Smith & Lansman), 139
Cognitive software models
  arguments for use of, 139–141
  future influence of, 141–146
  history of, 137–139
  negative aspects of, 142–143
  and other theoretical models, 135–137, 139, 141, 144–146
  overview of, 17–19, 134–135
  in specific software, 58–59, 137, 141
Colab tools (software), 80
College Composition and Communication, 149
College English, 124, 149
Collier, R., 80
Comments (software), 58, 80–81, 137, 153
Compact disc technology, 81–82
Composition
  cognitive models in, 134–135
  in general, 1–4, 94–96, 148–151
  hypermedia in, 125–127, 150
  in motivating students, 5–6
Composition theory
  diversity in, need for, 135–137, 141, 147
  general influence in CAC, 89, 93–94
  and hypertext, 125–127, 145
  See also Cognitive software models
Computer-Aided Composition (CAC). *See* CAC (Computer-Aided Composition)
Computers
  basic principles of, 13–14
  history of, 13, 129
  IBM PCs, 51, 76–77, 79
  Macintosh, 76–77, 82, 100, 110
  in schools, statistics on, 3, 122–123
  SUN workstations, 78
  Xerox 118 Dandelion, 86
  See also Programming; System architecture
Computers and Composition, 5, 53, 249
Computers and Writing Conference, 5, 115, 139–140, 144
"Computer Writing Facilities: The State of Art" (Collier), 80
CONDUIT consortium, 32, 101–105, 114
Confer (software), 16, 70, 72, 79, 83, 84–87
Conference on College Composition and Communication (CCCC), 45, 46, 115
Copy protection, 101
Cornell University, 34, 39–41
Corporations
  aspects of collaboration with, 130–133
  funding from, 40, 64, 97, 98, 131
Costs, examples of, 64, 96. *See also* Funding
Coulter, C. A., 6
Create/Recreate (software), 34
Creative Problem-Solving (software), 34
Creative Strategies Research International, 111
CSILE (software)
  description of, 59, 109, 144, 153, 154 (fig.), 156
  development of, 59, 62, 128
  funding for, 64, 97, 131

Index

networking with, 80

Daedalus Group, 42, 46–52, 115–117, 121–122, 131
  Daedalus Instructional System, 43, 48, 50–51, 116
  53rd Street Writer (software), 105, 106
Daiute, C., 6
Dalton, D. W., 6
Data abstraction (object-oriented programming, OOP), 69–72, 112–113, 122
Davis, Stuart, 34, 36, 99, 100
Declarative knowledge, 16, 17, 85
Deconstruction, 126
Delaney, Paul, 125–126
Department of Defense (DOD), 133
Derrida, Jacques, 126
Design/development, of software vs. academic work, 116–117, 121–122, 123
  collaboration with programmers in, 28–31, 38, 68
  definition of, 21
  programming expertise in, 30–31, 48, 91
  See also Programming; *names of specific models*
DiPardo, Anne, 74, 110
DiPardo, Mike, 74, 110
Direct-mail marketing, 115
Discipline, use of networks for, 130
Discourse Detective (software), 111
Diversity in theory, 135–137, 141, 147
DOD (Department of Defense), 133
Doheny-Farina, Stephen, 65, 148
DOS (disk operating system), 111, 122, 128
Duling, R. A., 6

EDUCOM
  Academic Software Development Survey, 41, 52, 87–88, 96, 99
  NCRIPTAL/EDUCOM Award for Outstanding Software, 41, 43, 90
Eisenstein, Elizabeth L., 2
Elbow, Peter, 6, 25, 139, 147
Eldred, Janet M., 126–127, 137
Electronic communications, 81, 124
ELIZA (software), 85
"Empirical Explorations of the Logic Theory Machine: A Case Study in Heuristics" (Newell & Simon), 18
Encyclopedia of English Studies and Language Arts, 149
ENFI system (software), 80
English Coalition Conference, 147
English departments, recognition from, 88–93, 96
Entrepreneurial design group model
  definition of, 23–24, 42
  description and examples of, 42–52
  funding in, 50–51, 57, 97, 115–116
  future of, 115–117, 121, 123
  reward and recognition in, 24, 52, 121
  user input and revision in, 50, 51
Essay Writer (software, later *The Writer's Helper*), 131. See also *The Writer's Helper* (software, formerly *Essay Writer*)
Evaluation of CAC programs, 91–92, 149. *See also* User input and software revision
Executive Communications, 54
Eyeball (software), 34

Feigenbaum, Edward, 138
53rd Street Writer (software), 105, 106
FIPSE (Fund for Improvement in Post-Secondary Education), 93, 97, 106, 114
Flower, Linda, 17, 58, 138–139, 146
Folio (software), 74
Fortune, Ron, 110–111, 127, 128, 147

Forum (software, later *Interchange*), 47, 49. See also *Interchange* (software)
Frames, cognitive, 68–69
FREE (software), 6, 25, 33, 137
Freewriting, software for
  FREE, 6, 25, 33, 137
  Prewrite, 26–29, 31–33, 68, 97, 137, 140, 157, 158 (fig.)
Fund for Improvement in Post-Secondary Education (FIPSE), 93, 97, 106, 114
Funding
  from corporations, 40, 64, 97, 98, 131
  for entrepreneurial design groups, 50–51, 57, 97, 115–116
  ethics in, 133–134
  general discussion of, 21, 96–98
  and impact of technology, 67
  for lone developers, 32, 97
  from military organizations, 64, 97, 133–134
  for professional developers, 52–53
  for research-based design teams, 22–23, 64, 97–98, 134
  for small design groups, 23, 36, 39–40, 41, 97, 114

Gaither, G., 41, 88. See also EDUCOM, Academic Software Development Survey
General Problem Solver (information-processing system), 138
General Problem Solving (GPS) theory, 18
Giansiracusa, Robert, 54–55
Gibson, Jim, 34
Giesler, Cheryl, 58
Grammatik (software), 137
Guide (software), 74

Haas, C., 6, 129
Hairston, Maxine, 135
Hannafin, M. J., 6
Hardware. See Computers; System architecture
HarperCollins publishers, 105–108

Havelock, Eric A., 2
Hawisher, Gail E., 6, 149
Hayes, John R., 6, 17, 58, 138–139
HBJ Writer (software), 118
Hepler, Molly, 103–104
Hobsbawm, E. J., 150
Humanistic perspectives, 94–96
HyperCard (software), 31, 73, 74, 110
Hypermedia/hypertext
  authoring systems using, 31, 72–76, 110–111
  and composition theory, 125–127
  definition of, 73
  general impact on composition, 95, 125, 150
  hardware requirements for, 78
  in specific CAC software, 34, 43, 50, 141
HyperTies (software), 74
HyperWord (software), 74
HyperWriter (software), 74

IBM
  and CAC development, 51, 111, 132
  funding from, 64, 131
  Interleaf Publisher (software), 79
  personal computers from, 51, 76–77, 79
ICAC (Intelligent computer-aided composition), 83–85
ICON computer, 128
Ideolog (software, later *Mindwriter*), 45. See also *Mindwriter* (software, formerly *Ideolog*)
Ideological biases, 128–130
InfoWorld, 53
Institutio Oratoria (Quintilian), 2
Intelligent computer-aided composition (ICAC), 83–85
Intelligent Systems Branch of the Air Force Human Resources Lab, 16
Intelligent Tutoring Systems (ITS), 15, 17, 83
Interchange (software, formerly *Forum*)
  description of, 42–43, 74, 137, 155 (fig.), 156–157

development of, 42, 46–50, 66, 74, 77
networking with, 77, 80
Interleaf Publisher (software), 79
Intertextuality, 126, 127, 145
ITS (Intelligent Tutoring Systems), 15, 17, 83

Jobs, Stephen, 147
Johnson-Laird, Philip, 68
Jones, Robert Alun, 82, 149–150

Kaplan, Howard, 6
Kaplan, Nancy
  on future of writing instruction, 2, 109, 128, 129, 134
  Prose (software) by, 34–42, 51, 97, 99–101, 113, 157
Kaufer, David, 60–61
Keane, D., 41, 88. *See also* EDUCOM, Academic Software Development Survey
Kemeny, John, 25
Kemp, Fred
  on future of writing instruction, 126, 128, 139, 142
  in software development, 30–31, 42–49, 66, 116, 121–122
  See also Daedalus Group
Kinko's Academic Software Exchange, 99
Kinneavy, James, 44
Klein, Sheldon, 17
Knowledge, in programming
  declarative, 16, 17, 85
  metatheory for, 17
  procedural, 14–16, 17
  qualitative, 16–17, 85

Landow, George P., 125–126
Lanham, Richard, 124–125
LANs (Local-area networks), 80
Lansman, M., 139
Laub, L., 81
Lewis, Dorothy Ohl, 22, 42
LISP (programming language), 25, 54, 86–87
Literacy, new, 125–126
Literary Machines (Nelson), 95–96
"Little" programs, 109–110, 119, 140

Local-area networks (LANs), 80
Lone developer model
  definition of, 22, 33
  description and examples of, 25–34, 54
  funding in, 32, 97
  future of, 75, 109–112, 121, 122, 123
  reward and recognition in, 22, 34, 121
  user input and revision in, 31–32, 33–34
Lotus 1-2-3 (software), 134–135
Lunar (software), 83
Lunsford, Andrea A., 4, 5, 10, 124, 148

McDaid, John, 110, 127
McDaniel, Ellen, 1, 92
McGraw-Hill publishers, 39, 51, 99–101
Macintosh computers, 76–77, 82, 100, 110
McKenzie, Alan T., 5
McLean, Bob, 59
McLuhan, Marshall, 2
Macroprograms, 118–119, 141
Manzelli, John, 75
Marginalized students, 127
Marketing of software
  by design groups, 114, 115
  by publishers, 103–104, 106–107
Martin, Joseph, 34, 36, 99, 100
Memory (computer)
  on CD-ROM, 81–82
  limitations of, 78, 79, 80, 86–87, 120
MicroSelect (network system), 129–130
MicroSoft *Windows*, 79, 103
Military organizations
  funding from, 64, 97, 133–134
  influence on system architecture, 129
MINA (software), 83
MindScape software publishers, 32
Mindwriter (software, formerly *Idealog*), 42, 45, 157
Minsky, Marvin, 68–69, 82–83

MIS Week, 54, 55
MLA (Modern Language Association), 4, 124
Modems, 81
Monitor screen size, 78, 79, 120, 129
Moore, M. A., 6
Moran, Charles, 3
Motivation, technology in, 5–6
Moulthrop, Stuart, 126

Nachman, Louis, 34, 36–37
NASA (National Aeronautics and Space Administration), 83, 133
National Council of Teachers of English (NCTE), 124, 149
National Science Foundation (NSF), 64, 97, 101
Natural language processing, 83–85
NCRIPTAL/EDUCOM Award for Outstanding Software, 41, 43, 90
NCTE (National Council of Teachers of English), 124, 149
Nelson, Ted, 73, 95–96
Networking
 and composition theory, 126
 distribution of software through, 99
 history of systems for, 128
 in impact on software development, 77, 79–81
Neuwirth, Christine
 cognitive theory in work of, 139, 141–142, 143
 on funding, 97, 98, 133–134
 on impact of technology, 78
 on reward and recognition, 64–65
 in software development, 57, 58, 59–61, 78, 80–81
Newell, A., 18, 138
New literacy, 125–126
Nodes, in hypermedia, 73
North, Stephen, 136, 139–140
Notes (software), 58, 60, 78, 137, 141, 157
NSF (National Science Foundation), 64, 97, 101

Object-oriented programming (OOP), 69–72, 112–113, 122
Odell, Lee, 65, 148
Office of Naval Research (ONR), 97, 133
Ohmann, Richard, 128
"On Computable Numbers, with an Application to the *Entscheidungsproblem*" (Turing), 13
Ong, Walter, 1–2
ONR (Office of Naval Research), 97, 133
OOP (Object-oriented programming), 69–72, 112–113, 122
Operating systems. *See* System architecture
Organize (software), 34, 36–37, 99, 101, 140, 157
OS2 (operating system), 79
Ownership of software, 49

Panopticon, Bentham's, 130
Paradigm shift, in composition theory, 135–136
Parlett, James
 and artificial intelligence, 83, 84–86
 Confer (software) by, 16, 70, 72, 79, 83, 84–87
 on future of CAC, 118–119, 121–122, 137
 in software development, 42, 70, 72, 79
 See also Daedalus Group
PASCAL (programming language), 48
Pattern matching in artificial intelligence, 85–86
PC Week (magazine), 54, 55
Piracy, 101
Polson, Martha C., 15, 17
Prep Editor (software), 157
Prewrite (software), 26–29, 31–33, 68, 97, 137, 140, 157, 158 (fig.)
Prewriting, software for
 Organize, 34, 36–37, 99, 101, 140, 157
 Prewrite, 26–29, 31–33, 68, 97, 137, 140, 157, 158 (fig.)
Problem-solving software models, 138

Index

Procedural knowledge, 14–16, 17
Process approach to composition, 135–136
Processing speed, 78, 79, 80, 120
Profession, 124
Profession 91, 5
Professional software development model, 24, 52–57
Programming
  declarative knowledge in, 16, 17
  hired programmers for, 28–30, 31, 38, 68
  with hypermedia authoring systems, 31, 72–76, 110–111
  with OOP (Object-oriented programming), 69–72, 112–113, 122
  procedural knowledge in, 14–16, 17
  qualitative knowledge in, 16–17, 85
  See also Programming languages
Programming languages
  general impact of, 12, 67–68
  impact on lone developers, 25
  natural language processing, 83–85
  specific languages, 25, 48, 54, 86–87, 103
Prose (software), 34–42, 51, 97, 99–101, 113, 157
Publication of software, 98–108
  by CONDUIT consortium (not-for-profit), 32, 101–105, 114
  by HarperCollins, 105–108
  by McGraw-Hill, 39, 51, 99–101
Public domain software, 114

Qualitative knowledge, 16–17, 85
Quintilian, 2

Rasche, Robert, 34
Recognition. *See* Reward and recognition
Research-based design teams
  and cognitive models, 135, 141–146
  definition of, 22–23, 57, 65
  description and examples of, 57–65
  funding for, 22–23, 64, 97–98, 134
  future of, in general, 117–120, 122, 135
  reward and recognition for, 23, 64–65, 87, 118, 121
  user input and revision by, 61–63
Revision, computers for, 6, 35–36, 38. *See also* User input and software revision
Reward and recognition
  from English departments, 88–93, 96
  for entrepreneurial design groups, 24, 52, 121
  general discussion of, 21, 87–96
  for lone developers, 22, 34, 121
  for research-based design teams, 23, 64–65, 87, 118, 121
  for small design groups, 23, 40–42, 113, 121
Richardson, Kim, 105–108
Robotel, 129
Rodrigues, Dawn, 34, 146
Rodrigues, Ray J., 34, 146
Ross, Donald, 34, 74
Royalty payments, 107

Scaffolding, software for, 58
Scardamalia, M., 58, 136, 139, 140
Scholar project, 16
Schools, statistics on computers in, 3, 122–123
Schwartz, Alan, 28
Schwartz, Helen
  on Carnegie Mellon, 143, 144
  Discourse Detective (software) by, 111
  on future of CAC, 111–112, 143
  Organize (software) by, 34, 36–37, 99, 101, 140, 157
  SEEN (software) by, 30, 51, 99, 104–105, 112, 114, 137, 157–158
  on software development, 72
Schwartz, Mimi, 24, 26–29, 31–33, 67–68, 113

Prewrite (software) by, 26–29, 31–33, 68, 97, 137, 140, 157, 158 (fig.)
Screen size, 78, 79, 120, 129
Second National Survey of Instructional Uses of School Computers, 3
SEEN (software), 30, 51, 99, 104, 112, 114, 137, 157–158
Selfe, Cynthia L.
  as editor of *CCCC Bibliography*, 149
  on future of writing instruction, 126, 127, 129, 130, 144–145
  on reward and recognition, 88–89, 92, 93–95, 96
  on software development, 25–26, 57, 68
  Wordswork (software) by, 30, 34
Shirk, Henrietta N., 127
Short, Doug, 132
Simon, H. A., 18, 138
Simon, Jane Fitz, 69
Simulation programs, 138
Situational analysis, 144
Small design group model
  definition of, 23, 41
  description and examples of, 34–42
  funding in, 23, 36, 39–40, 41, 97, 114
  future of, 75, 112–115, 121
  reward and recognition in, 23, 40–42, 113, 121
  user input and revision in, 38–39
Smith, Catherine, 111, 144
Smith, John B.
  on cognitive basis for CAC, 139–141, 144
  on costs, 23, 97, 98
  in development of software in general, 57, 58
  on future of CAC, 119
  See also *WE* (*Writing Environment*, software)
Snow, Charles Percy, 95
Social aspects of writing, 18–19
Social constructivist theory, 127, 128
Social-epistemic theory, 145
Software
  corporate influence on, 127–132
  military influence on, 133
  ownership of, 49
  See also Design/development, of software; Programming; Technology, impact on software; User input and software revision; *names of specific programs*
Speed, of processing, 78, 79, 80, 120
Spicer, Donald Z., 73, 75–76
StorySpace (software), 74
Strickland, James, 6, 25, 28, 33
SUN workstations, 78
Supercard (software), 74
Swimming above the Black Line (Schwartz), 26
System architecture
  ideological biases in, 128–130
  impact on software development, 76–79
  memory, 78, 79, 80, 86–87, 120
  processing speed, 78, 79, 80, 120
  screen size, 78, 79, 120, 129

TASP (Texas Assessment of Skills Proficiency), 121
Taylor, Paul
  on academics vs. software design, 116
  on impact of technology, 67, 87
  in software development, 42, 45–52, 66, 77
  See also Daedalus Group; *Interchange* (software)
Teacher's role with CAC, 120, 130, 146–148
Technology. See Composition, impact of technology on; Computers; Software; Technology, impact on software
Technology, impact on software
  artificial intelligence in, 82–87
  CD-ROM in, 81–82
  funding in, 67
  hypermedia in, 72–76

Index 187

networking in, 79–81
object-oriented programming (OOP) in, 69–72, 112–113, 122
overview of, 67
programming languages in, 67–68
system architecture in, 76–79
Telecommunications, 81
Texas Assessment of Skills Proficiency (TASP), 121
Texas Technological University, 121
Textbook publishers
  HarperCollins, 105–108
  McGraw-Hill, 39, 51, 99–101
Therborn, Goran, 128
Thoughtline (software), 25, 53–56, 82, 83, 115, 137, 158–159
ToolBook (software), 31, 74, 79, 111, 128
Turbo Pascal (programming language), 25
Turing, Alan M., 13

Ultimedia system, 111
United States Air Force, 16, 133
United States Army Research Institute, 64, 133
United States Department of Defense (DOD), 133
United States Office of Naval Research (ONR), 97, 133
University of Akron, 96
University of Illinois at Urbana-Champaign, 82
University of Iowa, 101
University of Maine, 92
University of Minnesota, 110
University of North Carolina at Chapel Hill, 57, 58
University of Texas at Austin, 43, 49, 52, 113, 131
User friendliness, design for, 29
User input and software revision
  definition of, 21
  by entrepreneurial design groups, 50, 51
  by lone developers, 31–32, 33–34
  by professional software developers, 53, 54–56

publishers in, 100–101, 102–103, 104–105
by research-based design teams, 61–63
by small design groups, 38–39

Van Neumann, John, 13
VIEWS (software), 74

Wadsworth publishers, 100, 101
Wahlstrom, Billie, 34
WE (*Writing Environment,* software)
  cognitive models for, 139, 141, 144
  description of, 13, 18–19, 62–64, 109, 137, 141, 144, 159
  development of, 59, 62–64, 78
  funding for, 133
  in future of CAC, 109, 119
Weizenbaum, Joseph, 13, 14, 85
What Is English? (Elbow), 147
Windows (operating system), 79, 103
Winograd, Terry, 84
Witte, Stephen, 136–137
Wood, John, 71
Woodruff, Earl
  cognitive theory in work of, 139, 144
  on funding, 64, 97, 98
  on future of CAC, 110, 145–146
  in software development, 57, 59, 62
Woods, William, 83
Woolley, W. C., 6
Word-processing programs, 3–4
Wordswork (software, formerly *Wordsworth II*), 30, 34
Wresch, William
  on collaboration with corporations, 131–132
  on future of CAC, 113, 119–120
  on reward and recognition, 89–90, 93
  on technological impact, 73
  See also *The Writer's Helper* (software, formerly *Essay Writer*)
Writers' Craft, Teachers' Art (Schwartz), 26

The Writer's Helper (software, formerly *Essay Writer*)
  award won for, 90
  commercial success of, 89, 97
  description of, 118, 159
  funding for initial development of, 131
  publication of, 51, 99, 101–105, 114
  Stage II, 103
Writing. *See* Composition, impact of technology on; Composition theory
Writing environments, 109–110, 118–119, 140–141. See also *WE* (*Writing Environment*, software)

Writing for Many Roles (Schwartz), 26
Writing without Teachers (Elbow), 25

Xerox 118 Dandelion computer, 86
Xerox Palo Alto Research Center, 80
Xpercom company, 52, 56. *See also* Burns, Dan

Young, Richard, 133–134, 135–136

Zimmerman, Muriel, 125